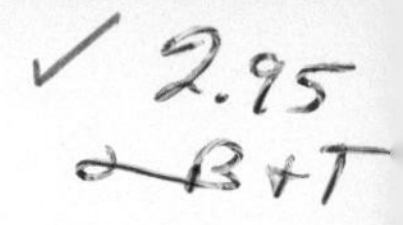

WHAT IS REAL IN CHRISTIANITY?

DAVID L. EDWARDS

THE WESTMINSTER PRESS
Philadelphia

PUBLISHED BY THE WESTMINSTER PRESS®
PHILADELPHIA, PENNSYLVANIA

PRINTED IN THE UNITED STATES OF AMERICA

Library of Congress Cataloging in Publication Data

Edwards, David Lawrence.
What is real in Christianity?

Bibliography: p.
1. Apologetics—20th century. I. Title.
BT1102.E29 201'.1 72-6337
ISBN 0-664-24964-7

TO MARTIN

WITH BEST WISHES FOR A LIFE

LIVED MOSTLY IN THE TWENTY-FIRST CENTURY

ACKNOWLEDGEMENT

The biblical quotations in this book are taken from the New English Bible, second edition © 1970 by permission of Oxford and Cambridge University Presses.

Previous versions of Chapters 6 and 10 appeared in the *Church Times* and in *Common Ground*, the journal of the Council of Christians and Jews, respectively, and I am grateful to the Editors for permission to use this material.

CONTENTS

PREFACE

This short, non-technical book attempts to be both honest and constructive. It has been written urgently, because the crisis confronting Christianity is very great. For years now I have been immersed in the discussion of the twentieth century's challenges to the Christian tradition. I have talked about the problems with many people as a college chaplain and as a parish priest. From 1959 to 1966 I was a publisher of theological books, as Editor of the Student Christian Movement Press. Many of the books were scholarly, but one of them, Dr John Robinson's *Honest to God* (1963), sold a million copies and introduced a vast new public to the excitement of some of the ideas being debated by some of the scholars. That particular excitement has now died down, although I claim that *The Honest to God Debate*, which I edited in 1963, is still worth reading. But the serious debate has continued, and although I have ceased to be a full-time publisher I have been allowed to keep an active connection with the publishing of other men's books. In most weeks I have reviewed a new theological book in the London *Church Times*. In recent years I have grown more interested in the social background to the intellectual debate, and I wrote quite a large survey of *Religion and Change* published by Hodder and Stoughton as one of their 'Twentieth Century Studies' in 1969. I have also attempted to study the nineteenth-century background, particularly in work for my book on *Leaders of the Church of England, 1828-1944* (Oxford University Press, 1971). I may therefore be forgiven if I now claim to be acquainted with the controversy—and if I confess that many of the questions raised still perplex me, I have had my nose well rubbed in the difficulty of it all.

But I honestly do not think that the final result of all this debate ought to be total confusion. Some answers have begun to emerge as a result of the unquestionable sincerity and ability of the debaters. These are the answers which I try to pull together. I made previous attempts in *God's Cross in Our World* (SCM Press, 1963), *The Last Things Now* (SCM Press, 1969) and *Still I Believe* (BBC, 1969), but this attempt is much more general. The simplicity of these answers will probably irritate any scholars who do me the honour of looking at these pages, but I hope that such scholars may be irritated into making weightier contributions to the religious reconstruction which is so badly needed. I hope, too, that the very simplicity of my brief summary—written in a house in Westminster across the road from Parliament—may help some readers who are interested in the intellectual debate chiefly as it relates to practical life. I shall be happy if this book helps any reader to see for himself how he may keep his honesty and integrity but take a few steps forward through the confusion.

Like many others engaged in the religious quest, I feel specially grateful to those who have encouraged me to persevere. Among these are the congregations who have so patiently listened in Westminster Abbey and St Margaret's. The invitation to write this book came some time ago, but the difficulty of the project deterred me until I received invitations to give two series of lectures during the early months of 1972, one near Johannesburg to the Association of Southern African Theological Institutions and one in Stepney to the Anglican clergy working in East London. These were audiences which I could scarcely refuse, and I only wish I could have helped them more.

D.L.E.

I

WE ADMIT

I

A crisis faces Christianity as the last quarter of the twentieth century opens. There has naturally been a great deal of discussion about it among Christians, but the discussion has often been superficial.

This is not merely a crisis of numbers. The decline of churchgoing almost everywhere, the drop in church finances, the young men's flight from ordination, the other statistics of depression—these are realities which rightly alarm those who support organized Christianity, but they are not the basic problems. It would be possible to have a Church reduced in numbers but strong in spirit. After all, Christianity began with tiny numbers, with almost no full-time preachers and with no buildings of its own —but its confidence proved stronger than the Roman Empire's. The most vigorous expressions of Christianity often occur without much reference to the institutional activities of the Church, and when groups of Christians are effective these are often small. And, as a matter of fact, the Church is not doing too badly for numbers. We see this when we compare the Church's regular congregations with the groups meeting regularly for other serious purposes. The regular churchgoers are few, but fewer still are the people who bother to turn up at ordinary meetings connected with the political parties, local government, trade unionism or adult education. No, the slump in the outward prosperity of the Church is not the key issue.

Much of the discussion about the declining Church fastens on its irrelevance to current social problems. The Church is told that its leaders ought to throw themselves with more passion into the struggles of our time for a better society, and that churchgoers ought to give more time to social service in the neighbourhood. And almost everyone agrees that more involvement in ordinary people's problems is, indeed, a Christian's duty. But the Christian Church cannot be expected to justify its existence chiefly as a pressure group in politics or as an agency in social welfare. When people go to church, they do not go in order to be told how to vote or in order to be recruited into social work. The ineffectiveness of the Christian Church in such fields cannot be the *main* cause of its decline. And the Church's ineffectiveness ought not to be exaggerated. We see this when, after remembering the Church's inevitable limitations, we begin to count up the Christians who do exercise some influence on political and social problems, either by pronouncements or (more profitably) by personal service which gets no publicity. The official pronouncements of the churches on the great social questions of recent years have been, on the whole, wise—and what matters more, most of us know individual Christians whose contributions to society we greatly respect. The blockage which exists in many minds is an objection to the Christian Church's religious message—or at least, to the religious message as it has been reflected in teachings about the basic structure of society.

When the Church's crisis is discussed in church circles, it is often described as a crisis in loyalty. The real problem, it is said, is that people who belong to the Church nominally are not faithful enough, and that those who go to church regularly do not pray enough, or give enough, or work enough. This is the Right Wing assessment of the situation, as the lack of 'social relevance' is the Left Wing assessment. However, we may doubt whether a simply moral improvement is what is really needed to solve the problem which perplexes the Church. As it is, the Christian Church commands a measure of loyalty which is impressive. Millions of people retain much good will towards it. Among its regular supporters, dogged perseverance and much self-sacrifice are to be seen. Certainly no one with a knowledge of history would suppose that the moral tone of the Christian Church is generally lower today than it was in most previous periods. It is higher. The fundamental question is not about morals. It is about morale. The trouble is that Christians are not confident about the truth in Christianity.

This is a crisis of religious faith, and it goes deeper than any attempt to modernize the Church's language. Obviously such attempts are needed badly. The Bible was written long ago and far away, and much in it seems remote even when the Bible is translated into modern speech. Obviously, too, the language used in many church services, for example in the hymns, is old-fashioned, and people can sit or sing through it (if they are willing to come and to stay) without gathering what it means. For Christians who think about what they read and hear, the scenery of the Bible needs to be updated and the sacred phrases of the Church need to be translated into modern idioms—otherwise the world of the Bible will be a remote world to modern people, and the Church a museum. But criticism of the Church as being out of date should not make us forget that religion often appeals precisely because it is mysterious, because it has a long tradition behind it, because it deals with things which are not the first things one bumps into on the street. Some highly traditional religious institutions have in the past been highly popular. And anyway, in recent years the spokesmen of Christianity have done much to meet the criticism. New translations of the Bible and new religious books pour out. Preachers and writers are energetic in producing modern illustrations to explain the Bible's teachings.

Church services are being revised so as to be more intelligible, and among many other experiments popular music is being used. Although many in the churches are naturally conservative, the mass media want news and in many countries a good deal of coverage is given by the mass media to Christianity presented as news. Although many clergymen are remote, school teachers and youth leaders are naturally eager to be in touch, and in many countries a good deal of religion, as up to date as possible, is offered to the younger generation in school and out of it. In Britain, for example, television and the school have to a considerable extent replaced the local churches as centres of religion. Around the world, Christianity's style is being renewed. But still the basic problem remains. It is the problem of the credibility gap between the Christian message and the modern mind.

This gap is not going to be bridged by any slick presentation of the Gospel which does not deal with the serious problems involved. Most people are not such fools as to fall for that. Their real objection is not that Christianity is unfashionable. It is that Christianity seems untrue.

Thought is required to meet this objection, if it can be met. And by thought we do not mean slogans. The gap between the Christian Church and the modern mind is not going to be closed by using some new philosophical phrase as an alternative to the conventional image of the Christians' God, if that phrase is really no more than the intellectual equivalent of fashion-consciousness. A good deal of recent discussion among Christian theologians has concerned the possibility of replacing the popular picture of God, which is said to be one of an old man with a long white beard resting somewhere above the stars. Such discussion has been a useful reminder that the conventionally pious image of God was only an image. It has also been a healthy attempt to relate the inherited Christian tradition to contemporary ways of thinking. Sensitive and intelligent Christians have made this kind of attempt in every generation throughout the Church's history. But the discussion has often been ineffective outside the ranks of the full-time theologians, for the average person understands the old images of God better than he understands the new philosophical phrases. To the public, these phrases have seemed mere slogans. And people who are intellectually equipped to go deeper know that a theologian has to probe very deeply indeed if he is going to make an intellectually honest job of exploring philosophy. More is involved than taking over some impressive words in order to give a tired old religion an air of intellectual smartness. The gap between the Christian Church and the modern mind is deep enough to need something solid to fill it—if it is to be filled at all.

2

The basic problem is the decline in the traditional Christian beliefs about the supernatural 'other' world.

One change is simply that people are no longer so interested as they used to be in exploring another world which is said to exist above nature. It is true that interest in spiritualism, astrology, magic and the occult is still surprisingly widespread, but it is usually only spiritualism that is taken with a real and public seriousness. People's reading of the horoscopes in the newspapers, or of the frequent articles about witches, is almost always for amusement only; if they do take these interests seriously they are shamefaced about them, because they know they are irrational. And spiritualism has not succeeded in really persuading many people that it can supply much authentic information about the supernatural world. 'There may be something in it' is as far as most people will go—and they are not prepared to take much trouble to find out more. *This* life holds too many fascinations for modern people to want to devote much energy to supernatural explorations or speculations. Life here is often pleasant—let us enjoy it! It is often full of problems—let us solve those problems! It is full, too, of duties—let us do our best here, and leave the hereafter, if it is real at all, for some tomorrow! This is the general attitude of modern people, and it is not the attitude that one generally finds in history.

Of course in the old days people kept themselves extremely busy with the delights, problems and duties of everyday life, but usually they acknowledged the supremacy of the supernatural. While eating, drinking and being merry, or while soberly at work, they were very conscious that death was near, and they were highly interested in what they were taught lay beyond death. At least in theory, preparing for eternity was held to be the most sensible way of using the few years during which their bodies would be alive. The move away from all that is a basic psychological change. People, including good people, have grown more worldly, and they are not ashamed of it. Even religious people have in recent years often agreed that they were much more 'secular' in their interests than their fathers were.

The supernatural 'other' world, while it has become less interesting psychologically, has also become less important intellectually. When we who are modern ask questions about ourselves, we do not treat ourselves as if we were supernatural spirits, ghosts in a physical machine, souls in a material prison; we know that we are people, and that our personalities cannot be carved up into a supernatural 'soul' or 'mind' and a natural 'body'. When we ask questions about our environment, we do not expect answers which involve that 'other' world. When we plan jobs which need doing, we do not reckon with the possibility of interference from the 'other' world. For example, when we try to understand agriculture better and to grow bigger crops, we do not ask which magic spells are best. When we are ill, we do not ask anyone to expel a demon from us. We may be aware that a lot of people alive in our time do believe in demons and so forth—and that not all these people live in villages in Africa or India. But when modern people think seriously about the occult, it is in order to bring any reality there may be in the old beliefs into the scientific world-view. We hope that science will make sense of the occult, not that the occult will make nonsense of science. Of course in the old days people were very shrewd, and African or Indian villagers have a canny wisdom amid (what we regard as) their superstitions. But in contrast with past generations, and in contrast with the world of belief which still lingers, we are in a new position, for we rely on science, and we know that everywhere the advance of science has meant the retreat of the supernatural.

Another profound change has taken place. The world opened up by science is full of interest and opportunity—but in the scientific world-view man has lost the supreme place which many mythologies gave him in the days when people accepted the supernatural. This planet Earth is now known to be a pinprick in the fireworks display of the universe. The evolution of *Homo sapiens* from other animals is known to have been a last-minute, or last-second, development in the emergence of life on Earth. Evolution is known to have taken place through natural selection, by the survival of the fittest, or best adapted, after genetic mutations which were random and in most cases harmful. In the astounding view of the universe which science provides, human life can so easily seem an insignificant accident among the galaxies. Of course, in the old days people often felt themselves to be dwarfed by nature and to be powerless when disaster struck. They were often terrified, and fear drove them to appease the devils or to seek the favour of angry gods believed to be in control of nature. But at least people did almost always believe that nature was under some kind of control which was closely related—or could be closely related—to their own feelings and doings. That was what prayer was thought to be about, and such prayer was thought to be effective. The immensity of the cosmic spaces did not often frighten people in the old days. The sun, moon and stars were comfortably like ornaments on a roof just above their heads. They assumed that at the centre of the universe Earth had been designed to supply the wants of man, or at least to provide man with an edifying education. They believed that the first man had been proudly created by the miraculous intervention of divine hands, and that every baby wet from the womb was the image of God, a living reminder of the miracle of Adam. Now, if we make any claim to being educated, we have to live in a universe which looks very different. Modern man often feels like an actor who has just noticed that his audience has vanished. No wonder that he often asks what new kind of play he should perform!

Christianity has not found it easy to cope with this discouraging background—any more than it has found it easy to respond to the short-term benefits offered by science as distractions from the surrounding darkness. For Christianity's hope for man seems to be tied to the mythology of the supernatural. To put it frankly, Christianity seems to belong to fairyland. It seems to have no relation to the real world, which is often cruelly hostile to human values and hopes. This cruelty seems, however, to fit into the scientific world-view, which suggests that the whole universe is produced by spontaneous combinations of the elements making matter and of the genes making life: in a word, by chance. In a random universe cruelty seems natural, and the 'Almighty Father' of Christianity seems as real as Father Christmas.

The confusion of Christian belief under these challenges has been increased by the confusion caused by the beginnings of conversation between the world's religions. No longer is it possible for an educated person to consider one religion in isolation from all others. Some of the many faiths held on our small planet are older than Christianity. Some are rooted far more deeply than Christianity is. Some have replaced Christianity in areas where it used to be dominant. Non-Christian faiths contain so much spiritual nobility that only a fool will dismiss them as merely 'heathen'. On the other hand, it is naïve to think that they harmonize easily. Buddhism, for example, is a radical protest against Hinduism. Even in our time religious differences have helped to produce great bitterness. The conflict of Hinduism and Islam has been a factor in hatreds and in millions of killings in the twentieth century, and the contrast between Islam and Judaism has helped to bring war to Jerusalem. One of the few points on which all these non-Christian faiths are agreed is that Christianity's traditional claim to be the one true religion, the only reliable account of the 'other' world, is impertinent.

So no single religion is likely to have a monopoly of truth. Does *any* religion contain *any* truth? The present confusion on the religious scene has emphasized how hard it is to make sense of religious talk. The supernatural 'other' world is believed, even by those who talk freely about it, to be 'infinite' and 'ineffable'—while our words have been coined to talk about the things we touch and about the people we meet. What is to rescue God-talk from being a series of meaningless noises? Many people now ask that question. And people know that it is particularly hard to be rational when one is talking about the supernatural inside one particular religious tradition. One is almost bound to be the prisoner of the tradition. The pressures of orthodoxy are very strong, even if they come not through fear of an inquisition conducted by the religious Establishment but through a sentimental attachment to one's own background. It is easy to understand why, in this field so full of intellectual problems, many modern people prefer to keep silent about the supernatural.

3

But even these difficulties do not account for the full force of the rejection of Christianity by many modern people. These are intellectual difficulties, and no one should treat them lightly—but most people are not intellectuals, and in matters of religion even the intellectuals do not seem to be motivated chiefly by intellectual considerations. The notion that many people give up praying because of some book that has recently appeared is a theory which could only have occurred to the optimistic authors of books. If we seek to understand the anti-Christian feeling which is a real force in the modern world, we must turn to social and psychological history. What really matters to many people is that they feel that the traditional Christian belief in the supernatural 'other' world has been an obstacle to progress. This goes deeper than any complaint that the Church is not a political pressure group or a social welfare agency.

The modern world carries the scars of many battles against the Church's teaching about the supernatural. In the industrial society produced by the nineteenth and early twentieth centuries, organized Christianity seemed to be allied with the exploiters of the working class. Preachers threatened rebels, strikers or agitators with hell fire. God would punish those who did not agree to be kept in their proper 'stations' in this life, but would reward the meek with 'pie in the sky', thus saving churchgoers from the obligation to pay decent wages. In the expansion of Europe to exploit other continents, the Christian Church was allied with the colonialists. Missionaries sent the Eastern heathen to hell—where they would far outnumber any Western revolutionaries. Even when missionaries adopted a politer approach, the effect of their patronage was to undermine the self-respect of the 'native'. The ancient civilizations of India and China were despised. Tribal life in Africa was beyond the evangelist's comprehension. And all the time, the creed of the missionaries blessed the arms of the conquerors. The cross was carried by the Spaniards in South America, and the Bible was in the hands of the Puritans who took the land of the Red Indians. In our time the Bible has been used to justify white supremacy in South Africa and the United States. Christianity has been rejected by millions because it has become the religion of the rich man, and of the white man. For example, this is the reason why the very large network of Christian churches, colleges, schools and hospitals in China has been destroyed. Marxism has emphasized this rejection with a tremendous force, but the hatred of a 'supernatural' religion which was used as a cover for oppression is very strong among many non-Marxists.

The use of Christianity in oppressing the working class and the colonial peoples is now far less prominent, and the memories left by it will gradually grow less bitter. But a further problem arises for Christianity. It has become unpopular among many well-to-do people with white skins. There has been an immense psychological rebellion against Christianity in the lands which used to be called Christendom. The explanation is to be found in the feeling that, when the emphasis on the 'other' world flourished, the natural instincts were thwarted. Sinners and heretics were consigned to hell—but many modern people are proud to share those 'sins' and 'heresies' which were in fact the natural expressions of vigour of body and mind. Teachers and parents imposed a great burden of guilt on the functioning of man's sexual instinct. Other natural and clean pleasures of life were denounced or suspected by many Christians as distractions from the pilgrim's stony path. The Church fought bitterly in defence of its dogmas, and in defence of what often amounted to a Fundamentalist view of the authority of the Bible. The powers of the State were employed for centuries to torture and kill critics of the Roman Catholic Church or of the Protestant National Churches. Within the twentieth century states have imposed censorship at the bidding of church leaders. It is not surprising that many of those who have rejected Christianity have done so in defence of human freedom and dignity.

While Christianity has preached a supernatural love, it has often resulted in arrogance, with results which have shocked even Christians. The Nazis who exterminated six million Jews were of course not Christian believers, but they had been baptized, they were never excommunicated, and they could link their 'final' solution of the Jewish problem with centuries of a virulent anti-Semitism which both Roman Catholic and Protestant spokesmen had encouraged with religious emotions. The preachers who sent armies into action against their fellow-Christians (in Germany, for example, during the thirty years' religious war of 1618-48) admitted no doubt that God spoke through them and that supernatural armies encouraged their soldiers. The same arguments have been heard in Ireland (one of the areas in Europe where religious belief survives most strongly) during the 1970s. It can be demonstrated that other religions have also bred intolerance, and that the Christian crimes had a complicated social history behind them, but the record remains ugly. It is easy to see why many people believe that the real danger lies in the enthusiasm aroused by religion—and specially in the zeal with which Christianity has claimed to be the one and only revelation of the supernatural 'other' world.

Shame about this history has been one of the motives leading Christians in the twentieth century to get involved in the life of society on the side of the poor and the coloured, in the service of humanity without attaching any strings, and in defence of toleration. These better Christian attitudes have become widely known, and must have led many people to take a more favourable view of Christians. However, the improvement in the personal attitudes of Christians is not complete; some Christians, including some who attract much publicity, firmly retain reactionary attitudes. Nor is the improvement of personal attitudes to society the complete answer to the basic crisis now faced by Christianity, as is shown by the fact that people who admire this better kind of activity by Christians are seldom persuaded by it to return to the traditional fold. Many people still think that, however well some Christians behave, fundamentally Christianity is tied to belief in the supernatural 'other' world—and fundamentally this remains an obstacle to the development of the modern world.

4

Clearly the confusion in religious belief has altered Christianity's whole position. The criticisms just mentioned have been jumbled together. This was deliberate, because their impact has been felt as one general impact on the prestige of Christian doctrine. The old authority of the Bible has been shattered—and also the old authority of the Church, including (but this is a point not made so often by theologians) the traditional authority of theology as a science.

It is true that there are still Christians alive in the world who hold that the Bible was divinely inspired word by word without error; these are the Fundamentalists. It is also true that there are some very staunch upholders of ecclesiastical authority, and that some theological movements have had some highly enthusiastic devotees. In a time of confusion, these inflexible positions are bound to attract some recruits who think that holding such a position is still the only way of being religious. Among the conservatives are some Christians who deserve the highest honour for their personal qualities. But education is bound to destroy these defences of the old authority by showing that bishops, preachers and even theologians have made many mistakes. The vast majority of those influenced by modern education have already ceased to respect the Bible as they do respect scientific evidence (in theory, at any rate); and in practice they do not treat religious teachers as scientists of the supernatural. Even conservative Protestants are often now embarrassed by the tradition of calling the Bible infallible, just as Roman Catholics are embarrassed by the doctrine of papal infallibility. The whole dogmatic attitude—'believe it because I tell you so, and you can always trust me'—has lost credibility among Christians as among others. It is a massive change in the history of Christianity, and it sets the scene for everything that follows.

Instead of the old readiness to believe what one was taught about the supernatural, a modern person, including the modern-minded Christian, is mostly an agnostic. Although people still claim to experience the supernatural, it is clear that when they report their experience (even to themselves) they have to use symbols provided by the society around them. For example, a Roman Catholic seeing a vision of 'Our Lady' will see her like a statue in church, but a spiritualist who does not believe in God will experience psychic phenomena which do not include anything divine. The raw material of this experience, whatever it may be, has been thoroughly processed by human hands before being sold to others. People reflecting on these facts may still obstinately maintain that one particular type of experience does penetrate the mysteries, while all the other types are misleading, but usually people conclude that the supernatural has never been seen directly or fully. Man-made symbolism is, most people agree, inevitable. That may seem a modest admission, but it has vast consequences in practice. It results in scepticism about the accuracy of the very rich and complicated accounts of the supernatural which have been handed down to us from the past. This scepticism tears up many elaborate maps of the 'other' world. It dismisses legions of angels and devils, breaks up the furniture of heaven, and throws cold water on hell. It treats all the gods and goddesses without exception as mythological, and eats away the abstract systems of metaphysics like an acid. It says that man is a kind of advanced ape, not any kind of imprisoned angel. It may say that God himself is no more than a projection from man's imagination; if it refrains from saying this, it does insist that man cannot know anything about the home life of God. The inner essence of the divine is unutterable. (To be fair, we have to record the best mystics were saying this before modern scepticism arose.) If there is any value in the speculations about the supernatural 'other' world which have consumed countless hours in the history of religion, it is the value which can belong to an exercise of the imagination.

The modern attitude is also sceptical about attempts to trace supernatural interventions in the course of nature or of human life. People who think look for scientific explanations everywhere, and when puzzles remain they do not rush to fill the gaps in science by bringing God in. A God of the gaps is, anyway, always shrinking, for science's understanding of the regularities in the natural order is always increasing. The idea of a God who normally leaves nature to work according to its laws, but who intervenes fitfully, is ever-increasingly incredible. So is the idea of a God whose interventions are dramatic thunderbolts which everyone must admit to be divine. The modern attitude rules out reliance on miracles if by a 'miracle' is meant anything like this. And here is another great change in the history of religion. Traditionally many prayers have been made for miracles of this kind, ranging from a cure in a desperate illness to a fine day for the local church's fête. Modern people have various attitudes to the mystery which still surrounds their lives, but in practice modern people do not rely on such miracles.

The religion that survives the coming of science in educated minds (if any religion does) is a religion never contradicting science—and never claiming knowledge beyond science without explaining precisely what experience is held to justify such a very remarkable claim. And a religion which has been disciplined under the modern challenges is not only cool towards many traditional descriptions of the supernatural; it is also suspicious of many traditional feelings about nature. To be sure, the decline of the belief that man can understand the supernatural only emphasizes the importance of what man can understand, which is nature; and the decline of interest in the supernatural only emphasizes that man belongs to nature.

In a scientific age, if a healthy religion is possible it will take a passionate interest in nature, celebrating both nature and the natural sciences. What we have in mind is not that religion should cut itself off from these realities. It is simply that belief in God should acknowledge that it has little information about why the divine Creator in whom it believes created all that exists. Much of Earth is beautiful, and religious people who take a delight in this can well imagine God being even more delighted. But man now knows that the universe carries on existing 5,000 million light-years away from this planet. What man does not know is why it exists. Indeed, much that man sees on Earth seems to him cruel or pointless. Man's own planet produces earthquakes as well as sunsets, tornadoes as well as daffodils, animals hunting each other in the jungle as well as birds strutting on a dew-glittering lawn. And the sea, covering seven-tenths of the globe, has a life which does more than grow kippers for breakfast and wash sunny beaches. Religion should not pretend to understand this enigma completely. The attempts that have been made to find a clear religious explanation of every event and phenomenon in nature—for example, the attempt to show how everything was designed by God—led to much folly and some dishonesty. Nature as we see it is evolving, and its development may be in a direction we think right, but nature as we see it cannot be interpreted at every point by the religious conscience. Even that fraction of nature which is alive cannot be understood; for in its first 2,000 million years life has produced 500 million or more species, most of them now extinct. What religion can begin to explain, if it can explain anything at all, is the existence of man in these bewildering and astounding circumstances.

And even this limited topic of human existence cannot be covered in the old style of assurance. It is evident that religious talk about the mystery of human life is always symbolic. Christianity has used some symbols, basically those which one first-century Jew used. If Christians are to have the intellectual integrity which our scientific age demands, they have to think out the meaning of these symbols in relation to twentieth-century knowledge. And they have to be acutely conscious and ashamed of the tragic misuse of these symbols in order to fight the development of the modern world by justifying oppressive and subhuman practices in the name of the 'supernatural'.

II

WE ADMIRE

I

While traditional religion including Christianity has been in confusion, the modern world has developed with many brilliant successes. That may seem obvious enough; yet the temptation to concentrate on the world's weak points has been so strong for the adherents of the religions, including Christian churchmen, that the obvious now needs emphasis.

The majority of mankind now has a say in deciding its destiny. Under many régimes it is still a small say politically, and very few people are masters of their own situations in earning a living. Still, the general picture is one of some liberation. No tyranny can survive in the modern world without grand talk about democracy. No army can run a country without promising elections. No employer can exploit labour without maintaining that the wages he pays are the highest possible. No nation can hold down another without constantly reminding everyone that it was invited in. No race can treat another as subhuman without denying such a policy. These pretences are odious, but it would be worse if they were not thought compulsory—and in no previous period of the world's history were they so widely believed to be needed. Many hundreds of millions of people have, indeed, made solid and unprecedented advances during this century towards the freedom which is the almost universal theme of propaganda and advertising. The idea that a government must be responsible to its people is, in the setting of the history of the world, a new idea. The nervousness of the governing class is a new emotion. The near-complete collapse of colonialism is a new fact, and freedom from poverty is a new hope.

Equality is talked about today as never before. The obligation of the State to educate its citizens is everywhere acknowledged, although some states remain too poor to tackle the task and no state does so perfectly. At least modern people think that they ought to be, and can be, literate—an ambition beyond most of their fathers' dreams. Workers and peasants look to politicians and to their own unions to protect their interests, as their fathers could not look to their rulers, landlords or bosses. The drive towards equality is beginning, however slowly, to include the female half of mankind. Children are respected in a revolutionary way. Young people have money to spend as they like, and their parents are still not used to this new custom under which the prodigal son is based on home.

Because people now think that health is natural, hygiene and medical care are more widespread than ever before, although in many parts of the world they are still rudimentary. The capitulation of the centuries under disease and death is now rejected. Babies are expected to survive both birth and infancy. Great plagues, the scourges of history, have been prevented, and cures have been discovered for many previously terrifying diseases. Surgery performs daily miracles. In those areas where doctors are around the corner death has become so unfamiliar in real life that it has had to be brought back into the home by way of entertainment through television. Mankind's most urgent problem has become how to feed the extra mouths. In the determination to grow enough food a green revolution has transformed agriculture in prosperous countries, and is beginning to rescue the developing nations also. Mankind now has the technical resources to feed the present population of the world, and even to cope with some increase in the population. It also already has the power to limit births to acceptable numbers, and easier methods of birth control are being discovered. Meanwhile more than one industrial revolution has come and gone, making advanced economies grow fabulously and making the public in these countries irritated that it cannot get richer even more quickly, with the result that the public has insisted on being paid more anyway. The consequent inflation is evidently tolerable; otherwise it would not be tolerated. The economy is expected to sort itself out while the citizens of these affluent nations worry about slimming.

For the first time in history mankind is becoming mostly urban. All the problems which have resulted have not often produced a return to the fields except when the man who has made his money in the town chooses to spend it in the countryside. All the sufferings of workers uprooted from the soil and condemned to slums or shanty towns have not blotted out the ambition for a richer life in the city. In many areas, even if improved agricultural technology had not reduced the demand for labour, this ambition would have emptied the countryside. The nostalgia for grass has created the suburbs, and the suburbs have created now familiar human problems, but still suburbia, as the attempt to get the best of both the urban and the rural worlds, is part of the ambition to build a thoroughly enjoyable family life and civilization for the millions instead of for the few. The appetite for consumer goods, created by the city-based industries, is increasingly being satisfied by them. This is not the highest form of heroism, but it is difficult to believe that the possession of consumer goods is what degrades a man or woman. It is perfectly true that immense sums need to be spent on new housing and on public facilities in our cities, if public squalor is not to accompany private affluence. But if the economic base of our civilization grows, immense sums will be available. The children of the men whose contemporaries have reached the moon ought to be able to clear many slums.

It has been inevitable that in this transformation of humanity's conditions the emphasis has been solidly material, physical and technical. Such an investment of skills has already paid high dividends, and promises an even greater yield. It has, no doubt, also been inevitable that the commentary coming from religious circles has been, for the most part, cold. The wickedness of the modern world has been stressed, and every kind of critic of society has been welcomed as an ally. What the world has achieved has been dismissed as materialism. But we may observe that when the churches become refuges from the sheer evil of the modern city, they are liable to be embarrassed by their God and their Jesus. If, as Christians claim, the Father created the universe where Earth is a small suburb, he must be a materialist on a scale past any modern technologist's most intoxicated ambition. If he is the author of life, he must enjoy the physical beyond the stage which is usually regarded as polite. Jesus certainly drew down-to-earth conclusions from his belief in such a God. In the only sermon he preached in Nazareth, he is reported to have used a quotation from the only literature he knew, the Old Testament, to explain why he was no longer a village carpenter. His mission was

> to announce good news to the poor,
> to proclaim release for prisoners and recovery of
> sight for the blind;
> to let the broken victims go free,
> to proclaim the year of the Lord's favour.

This revolution of a poor man's expectations, this opening of the eyes to a future of freedom, is one of the realities of our time. Believers in God ought not to be as sure as many of them seem to be that these are years of the Lord's disfavour.

2

But to describe the twentieth century as an age of complete materialism is mere talk. Many facts point in another direction.

The two world wars could not have been fought had not millions of ordinary people been prepared to sacrifice every liberty and comfort, and life itself, for the sake of the causes propounded to them by their leaders. Military conscription was accepted, but civilians were also willing to throw themselves into the war effort. On neither side was there much pressure for peace until the very end. No previous century witnessed soldierly courage, or the stubborn refusal to surrender under adversity, in so many. After both wars there was a long sequel of privation, and after both wars the reaction came: disillusionment with wartime propaganda, anti-militarism and a massive turning to the pleasures of peace. But the heights to which human nature rose during the wars should not be forgotten in a time when idealism seems to be monopolized by pacifism. Nor should the sacrifices which made it possible for later generations to enjoy the pleasures of peace be too quickly washed away. And although it is easier to be grateful to those who at an appalling cost succeeded in overthrowing evil régimes, it is surely also possible to include the defeated dead in our memory of the pain in the two world wars, through which the world where we live was born.

It is easy to say that in our post-war world each man seeks only his own comfort. In fact, however, the world emerging from the great wars has still been swept by the passions of patriotism. The nations entangled in the wars have remained acutely conscious of their identities in peacetime, but others have copied them. The collapse of the Austro-Hungarian Empire in 1918 produced a litter of new European nations, and the damage done by the Second World War to the colonial empires has been followed up by nationalism remaking all Asia and Africa. Not one of these nationalisms would have been possible as an emotional force without the people's willingness to subordinate private interests to nation-building. Sometimes this willingness has been enforced, but even police states depend on the acquiescence of public opinion and often the willingness has been enthusiastic. The supremacy of the State over the individual for the sake of the general good has, of course, been preached and (normally) believed as the orthodoxy of the thousand million people now living in Communist nations.

It is easy to say that, because a man regards his country as part of himself, nationalism is part of self-interest. But the twentieth-century nation has operated in a time of a real fervour for social justice, outside as well as within the Communist camp. The extension of the social services at the taxpayers' expense has made systematic what had previously been left to charity. In many nations the Welfare State, or something approaching it, was created amid sincere idealism, and there is no reason why it should now be viewed with a complete cynicism. Indeed, there is much evidence that, although ours is an age of nationalism, the blend of self-interest and compassion that made the Welfare State has been extended beyond national frontiers. For the first time in history rich nations have acknowledged an obligation to help poor nations to grow economically. Although such aid has often been grudging in practice, it remains the equivalent of voluntary taxation. The 'Welfare World' is very far off, but the period when the idea caught on should not be dismissed as one unable to dream.

It is easy to stress the great dangers that remain. The armaments which have come to seem part of any respectable nation's furniture (partly because of the effect of the world wars) present dangers which are obvious but which certainly deserve all the attention they so often get, because so little has been done to lessen those dangers. Our age has a strong taste for violence (again, partly as a result of the wars) and persists in gunmanship in the streets even if it is too frightened to fire off the intercontinental missiles. The nations whose economies are growing are polluting and exhausting Earth's natural resources with a rapidity which is likely to arouse the anger and contempt of future generations. The aid to poor nations is far from enough, and the population explosion makes famines real possibilities once again. The bitterness between the races is already enough to tear humanity apart, and may grow. All this must be acknowledged. But some hope is possible because all this *is* acknowledged—so often that the protests against war, violence, pollution, poverty and racism become boring. The conscience of our society cannot fairly be called silent. Our age may be committing suicide, but if so it is explaining why and how endlessly before it does it. More probably our age is pulling itself back on the brink of disaster. People know that it is technically possible to survive, and the very knowledge causes the world-wide protest against the present drift to death.

It is easy to complain that public affairs get too much publicity in our highly political age, with the result that the life of the spirit is impoverished. It is, however, a fact that the mass media have opened many minds previously very narrow, not only to the dangers and disasters of our time but also more subtly to new people, new things, new places and even sometimes new ideas. The level at which this is done is usually trivial, yet it is done, and it constitutes an unparalleled education of mankind. Many modern novels and dramas, including some films, enlarge the sympathies at a deeper level. So do the sciences dealing with man himself. It is true that there has been a decline from the glory of the nineteenth-century novel, and that psychology and the other human sciences are still in their infancy, but authors reaching the twentieth-century public have led countless expeditions to explore these forbidden territories of the heart, with the result that human unhappines is understood (if not cured) as in no previous period. Ours is an introspective age, but that is not all that should be said about it. Music has always been a power taking people outside themselves, and it is a fact that music—and not only pop—has been enjoyed far more widely in our time than in the times of the classical composers. Nor has our time been destitute of serious composers. Nor has our time failed to appreciate the visual arts; on the contrary, the masterpieces which were previously enjoyed only by a very few are now known to millions through museums or reproductions. Nor has our time lacked major artists. And when assessing the cultural situation, it is only fair to remember that universal education has only just begun to bite into the poverty of the mind, while the new advances of mechanization and automation in industry (including agriculture) have only just begun to reduce the exhaustion of labour. What flourishes now in 'culture'—and much does flourish—is a foretaste of what a more educated and leisured generation could create.

Capitalism exploits sexual suggestiveness in order to get money out of young people; contraception encourages young people to enjoy more physical thrills; and naturally people who have been trained in the decencies of religion (or of Communism) are shocked. Sexual permissiveness is part of the life-style of the new generation which is hungry for experience and able to seize it, and naturally older people are conscious of the gap between the generations. In modern society these are serious, as well as famous, problems. Critics of a degenerate age should, however, reflect that many modern trends have strengthened family life. Young people still usually honour marriage as the crown of sex. Fewer marriages are arranged by parents, and fewer marriages are reluctantly entered because a baby is on the way after a casual affair. The greater equality between men and women has made marriage and child-rearing more of a partnership. The need to 'do it yourself', instead of bringing in a workman or doing without because of poverty, has led many to spend more time and find more satisfaction at home. That much-abused symbol and instrument of modernity, the television set, is domestic. Although more people than before avail themselves of the facilities for divorce—because most of the facilities are new—there is no evidence to suggest that more people are unhappy husbands or wives. The evidence suggests the contrary.

The younger generation, while depending on the progress made in these various directions, often rebels. That is, surely, as it should be. History is made by generations young, energetic, impatient and innovating for a time; and thanks to medicine and economic growth there are many more young people alive now than ever before, so that unprecedented energies, protests and novelties are to be expected. But the younger generation belongs to the time against which it protests. We need not be starry-eyed about the young to see that it is part of the achievement of the twentieth century to have bred a generation so fine—stronger in their bodies and therefore prouder of them, technically often cleverer than their fathers, often with a keener sense of social justice, with a firmer grip on the simple necessities of peace and love, and with a less inhibited delight in life. In the more prosperous countries, whether capitalist or Marxist, a less materialistic generation is arising, partly because the advance of the surrounding economic system has reduced the need to be dedicated to hard labour and money-making. In the poorer countries there is often a great bitterness in the new generation, which sees the men in power so slow to respond to the real needs of the hour; but behind the bitterness is the conviction that with more modernization injustice could be put right, poverty conquered, and a less corrupt and more humane society established. And many in the younger generation, whether richer or poorer, are prepared to sacrifice selfish ambitions if they can be shown a spiritual reality worth contemplating, or if they can be offered a dynamic hope for society as a whole. Such a generation has the power to bring the world it wants closer to reality.

3

In response to the progress of the modern world, the Christian Church seems to have one duty. It is to celebrate. If, as Christians claim, every increase in man's creativity is due ultimately to a blessing from the divine Creator, it is evident that God has now done a great new thing. If, as the Bible teaches, God is active, so to speak visiting and rescuing people who depend on him, it is clear that God has done this again recently. In German Protestant theology there is a quaint distinction drawn between God's right hand and his left. With his right hand, God offers religious salvation. With his left hand, he works in a secular way. On such a theory the twentieth century is the great time of God's *left* hand. One duty of the Church in such a time is to take a delight and pride in man's new powers and to give thanks for the mighty new acts of God. To the Christian that will be a single duty. Surely the Church should be eager to be used by modern people as a means for arranging celebrations, and should contrive to give thanks when modern people have forgotten to celebrate.

But is this the Christian Church's only function?

III

WHY GO ON?

I

Most modern people are not totally bored by the religious question. Although religion is in disarray and retreat in the modern world, it survives on a massive scale and it does this because there are still many people alive to support it or at least to take an interest in it. Even if we were to exclude Africa, the Middle East, India and South East Asia from the discussion as not being 'modern'—but would that be completely fair?—we should still have to reckon with many millions of adherents of religion, and of Christianity at that, in North and South America, Europe and Australasia. And far larger numbers keep some sense of identity with the religious, and specifically Christian, tradition without being committed members of the Church; while being, indeed, highly critical. Many public opinion polls taken in these vast areas have shown that only a small minority is prepared to state frankly and firmly that it has no religion at all. The man in the Western street still usually regards it as an insult if you tell him that he is an atheist. The younger generation would certainly be indignant if it were ever to be accused of having no soul.

Some intellectuals scoff loudly at this remaining sympathy with religion, regarding it as no more than the afterglow left by a dead faith in a secular society, and it is perfectly true that much of this 'afterglow' religion is muddled sentimentality. On the other hand, even sentimentality can show a man's real psychology. The average man is more religious than his intellectual critics are in his basic feelings. In a number of countries such as Britain he shows this by supporting the more or less compulsory arrangements which exist for the religious education of his children. Religious broadcasts and TV programmes still attract vast audiences. The newspapers reflect some popular interest in news about religion. Some books about religion sell widely. Some pop songs with a religious content are around the top of the charts.

Under Communist governments atheism is part of the philosophy of the State. But even in these countries religious belief survives on a scale which has alarmed Marxists—and not only in Eastern Europe. It is also fair to point out that, specially in Russia and China, Marxism itself possesses religious features. The position of Stalin in Russia, and of Mao in China, cannot be explained without recalling that propaganda previously characteristic of religion was employed in the glorification of a politician, the nearest parallel being the worship of the Roman and Chinese emperors as divine. Quite apart from the leadership cult, Marxism's vision of a perfect world, coming after the present time of troubles, has close parallels with the Jewish-Christian hope of the 'kingdom' of God. This hope reached Marx through his family (which had included many rabbis) and through the half-Christian philosophy of Hegel. The position of the Party in Communism is similar to the position of the Church in Christianity, while Marxism also has its sacred books. These features do not make the atheism which is a vital part of Marxism any less formidable, but they do mean that Marxism owes much of its success to its ability to meet needs previously catered for by religion. This is all that needs to be said if Marxism is thought capable of replacing religion. But if it is thought that Marxist doctrine will prove too narrow for the human spirit—and many signs already point that way—then the question remains: what will satisfy mankind's religious needs in a future which will have rejected large parts of Marxism as well as large parts of traditional religion?

This is a profound and urgent question. For throughout history the inspiration provided by religion has been vitally important in building and maintaining the quality of human life.

Religion has been man's main attempt to answer positively the questions about who he is and what he is to do. A convincing answer to such questions can release great energy into every part of the life of a society, for a firmly-held religious belief gives an individual both a strong sense of assurance and a strong sense of obligation. Christianity, for example, despite its defects and mistakes, has made a colossal contribution to civilization, because at its best Christianity has taught the dignity and duty of man with an infectious power. Even religions which seem to take a more gloomy view of the human condition, such as Buddhism in its earliest form, have exercised an incalculable influence enriching the societies in which they have been accepted. History shows repeatedly that a self-confident society accepts a heroic religion—or adapts an existing religion in a more cheerful direction (as has happened in the history of Buddhism). However, the assured society does not entirely create the happy religion, for the religion began in an austere style, with its saints and martyrs, in an obscure corner before the prosperous days came. When a particular account of reality taught by a religion begins to seem implausible, that doubt about a basic religious belief can undermine the assurance of the whole society which had accepted it.

If the doubt about religion is extensive enough, values are thrown into chaos and people no longer know where they stand. No doubt the society was already cracking up, and this confusion in the society undermined the religion; the religion and the society influence each other as they rise and decline. But often religion is one of the first foundations of a society to shake.

The question is now what, if anything, can replace the traditional religious foundations. That is a question troubling every area of the world where traditional religion is under challenge, but it is raised acutely in the 'post-Christian' areas where the basic values were built by Christianity.

Many novels, plays and films, and some paintings, explore this question, as do the existentialist philosophers. This commentary on our society by some of its most sensitive members is often bleak. These artists describe an existence without much meaning. Events have no real pattern of progress. What meaning there is in life is put there by the efforts of human beings to communicate with each other and to carve out together a life which will be good, or at least tolerable, in defiance of the absurd reality. But, tragically, people's passions and stupidity are such that they can manage very little in either communication or construction. They are doomed. Such is the despairing vision of life conveyed by many artists great and small. It is a vision which, no doubt, is caused partly by the artist's own sense of alienation from the main trends prevailing in a society concentrating on the goal of economic growth. But it is also a vision which, when offered, is accepted by many readers and audiences as deeply true. In fact, any more cheerful account of man's nature and destiny is compared with this one and is rejected as sentimental, although a passing glow about 'love' is pardoned in the young. And many people with no taste for such serious subjects seem to show that they, too, agree that life as a whole is more or less meaningless, for they often say that the only realistic course is to concentrate on today's work and today's pleasure in a spirit of crude selfishness and materialism. In practice many people are more idealistic and more tender than their basic philosophy would allow—which is why many of them still have some respect left for religion. But to them as to the artists, the truth about life is harsh.

This mood produces the profound and urgent question. What vision is to inspire the great energies which, beyond doubt, man needs to exercise if modern civilization is to be saved from disaster? We have already expressed our admiration of the energy with which our society has been warned about its dangers. We have expressed, too, our conviction that a new generation could tackle these problems with its increased scientific and economic resources. Many of the problems involved are technical, and if there was enough energy technical solutions could be found. But to have the means to solve a problem is not necessarily to have the will—as is known by a civilization which finds it impossible to give up cigarettes.

The question about the future of nuclear weapons—which may be reduced in number, but which will never be forgotten—is what vision of the family of man will prove stronger than the nationalisms which have so often produced war. If no such vision is available, people will have to continue to rely for centuries to come on the deterrent of mutual bluff always preventing aggression, and on there never being a serious accident—or they will have to accept a world government with an ideology consisting of little more than law and order, the ideology of tyranny. The question about the future of our cities is what vision of them will prove shining enough to awaken those who sleep in lethargy and selfishness. Otherwise the brutalizing effects of overcrowding will continue to grow, and the frustration and stress will breed more and more violence. The question about Earth's future is what reverence for nature—and for unborn generations who will need air, water, soil, living-space, fuel and raw materials

—will prove more powerful than human appetites and the get-rich-quick drive. If no such vision arises, one generation's greed will continue to rape Earth. Almost certainly the need to limit the world's population (at present doubling every thirty years or so) will result in compulsory birth control. But then the question will arise: in what spirit will the programme of population control be carried out? What vision of the lives of those who are to be allowed birth will replace the instinct to increase mankind? The question about the future of rich societies is what meaning will fill the leisure produced by machines doing work which used to be done by human hands and brains. If their leisure is empty, affluent people will die from the spirit's malnutrition. The question about the future of the poor countries is what vision of planetary justice will prove stronger than the selfishness of the rich man's club. For without a vision stronger than the pull of short-term economic advantages, the gap between the rich and the poor will be allowed to widen, joining the gap between white and coloured until the coloured poor take revenge on anything that may be left of the rich man's civilization after the other disasters—and then the coloured poor will find themselves no better off. Evidently, what is needed is an agreement among mankind about what is a reasonable standard of living, and an agreement that living consists of more than the infinite multiplication of the consumer goods seen in advertising.

Thus the future of our society depends on a revival of a vision of man's dignity and duty—the vision which has been provided by religion in previous societies. And more than a political renewal is needed; for while much self-restraint is urgent, so also is a deeper self-fulfilment. Religion says that the two go together.

The idea that a society can progress while individuals in it are trampled on or ignored is an idea which has appealed to many glory-drunk leaders of the twentieth century, but in each case their leadership has turned out to be a disaster. A society cannot be happier than its members. Within an effective vision of social justice there always has to be an insistence on the quality of the individual's life; the flavour of a society's happiness comes from a deep, spontaneous sense of purpose and joy in living, whatever obstacles the individual may face. Here again religion has provided the main inspiration in history, for the framework of meaning given by religion has included a definite place for the individual. And here again, the decline of traditional religion has led to a failure of nerve. It is a striking fact that the great increase in the material equipment for a happy life has so far not produced a great improvement in peace of mind. Churchmen are not the only people so concerned about the disadvantages of modern civilization that they need to be reminded about its good achievements. Many modern adults, the citizens of 'developed' countries, feel that their own lives are more or less pointless, and that material comforts do not console them enough. Few members of the younger generation—in East or West, North or South—hold such a society in respect.

All this is admitted very widely, even among those whose scepticism about traditional religion has caused its decline. Sometimes an attitude which can be called 'heroic materialism' is advocated as the answer. This involves an acceptance of the lack of meaning in life as a whole and a concentration on the material side, but it tries to include also a rebellion of the human spirit against this weight of purposelessness and materialism. Man is summoned to be a hero although his situation is thought to be tragic—like a doctor in a plague-ridden city. But it is hard to believe that such an attitude, however heroic, has provided the necessary inspiration in the past, or will provide it in the future. The encouragement which people have derived from religion has been gained from religion's teaching that *what ought to be* is also *what could be*, and is indeed in a real sense, up to a point, *what already is*. It remains a question: what will be the source of courage if this teaching is completely rejected?

Some philosophers and—more influentially—many dramatists have spread the vision of life as essentially a lonely affair. According to this vision, such meaning as there is in human life lies only in the fact that an individual can defy his doom, keeping his own integrity to the end. But most people find such a vision dismaying. Experience confirmed by psychology and sociology shows that, with the possible exceptions of the occasional genius or the mentally sick, people cannot face life alone but hope for fulfilment alongside others in harmony with a reality greater than themselves. Certainly religion when it has flourished has been a corporate, as well as an individual, activity. It has claimed to reveal *what could be* and *what already is* in a way that encourages people; and whether or not that claim was valid, it has on this basis brought people together in a shared faith and celebration. Once again we see that the problem now is whether a substitute can be found for traditional religion's inspiration of man in society.

Many people who know that materialism cannot satisfy the human spirit, and who also know that a man cannot stand alone, turn to a reality which they think does give meaning to life: the reality of 'love'. This is the theme of innumerable songs voicing a popular philosophy. But what is 'love'? The songs have concentrated on young sex. But, as many of the songs have said, that leaves the problem of inner loneliness more or less as it was—and accordingly sadness prevails. 'Love', to be satisfying beyond the physical thrills which are so easily obtained, seems to involve friendship, marriage and the whole life of society. That is why so many pop songs have pushed into areas traditionally covered by moral or spiritual teaching based on religion.

2

This question about the value of religion comes home to each of us directly, because for some practical purposes one has to make up one's own mind about religion. We may rightly insist on being agnostics about many traditional descriptions of the supernatural and about many traditional claims that the supernatural has intervened in nature and history, but are we to give any time at all to religious meditation about ourselves and our surroundings? And are we to allow religion any influence on our daily behaviour? We may rightly refuse to take literally all the traditional accounts of religious teachers such as Jesus, but what value do we place on the traditions about them, on their own teachings in so far as we can recover and understand these, and on their personalities? We may be rightly suspicious of the claims of religious institutions such as the Christian Church, but do we wish to see religion discouraged by the State? Do we wish the schools not to mention it? Do we hope that all its buildings will be deserted, apart from the tourist trade? And if some religion ought to survive, what ought its contents to be? We are right to be tolerant of our neighbours' views, but it is not charitable to be completely silent if considerable numbers of our neighbours, while apparently sane, insist on holding and spreading views which we believe to be false. In an appropriate way and at an appropriate moment, we ought to point out that they are false. We are right to refuse to impose any religious theory on the next generation, but what part of the heritage of religion are we willing to tell our children about, with what explanations?

For these reasons, many people today, while being agnostics about traditional descriptions of the supernatural 'other' world, are looking for a religion which will be real to them.

IV

RELIGION: VALUABLE?

I

It is time to state what is the value of religion. In the old days religion was so confident in its descriptions of the supernatural 'other' world, and was often so reactionary in practice, that it had to be criticized drastically when people achieved knowledge and freedom; and still in our time any honest people who remain religious have to say loudly and often what they admit was wrong in the past. But in these days religion is so confused that it is failing to make the contribution it could make to progress. Except in staunchly conservative circles which are too confident to be intelligent, religion tends to suffer from a failure of nerve. Thus in recent years some Christian theologians have argued that their creed had little or nothing to do with the general run of human religion. There has also been much discussion among theologians about the possibility of a 'secular' or 'religionless' Christianity, because (however devoutly religious the theologians who produce such ideas may be) that looks like the only decent clothing to put on Christianity when introducing it to the world. Religion must be wrapped up in newspaper. Some theologians have made brave efforts in this direction—only to find that the younger generation, conscious of the spiritual vacuum left by the collapse of the old beliefs, seems to be asking for something remarkably like religion.

In addition to celebrating the birth of the modern world, people who are both honest and religious now have a duty to say what can be gained from religion for the world's future—because the need for a new spiritual vision is so urgent that without a more effective contribution from those who have inherited religion, modern civilization will probably not have a future. The time has come to say something after the apologies. And what can be said is clear enough.

Although the spokesmen have so often been arrogant, many millons of people who have practised religion without making a fuss about it have shown a much more attractive attitude. Religion has made them humble, because it has persuaded them to seek wisdom modestly instead of being loud-mouthed in their own ignorant opinions, and when it has got them in this teachable frame of mind it has taught them how to live above the level of the animals. It has helped them to tame their instinct to rush to gratify every appetite as soon as it was felt, and it has even helped them to order their sexual appetites. It has enabled them to control habits which gave immediate physical pleasure but damaged body or mind. That is the reason why so many people have relied on religion against dehumanizing addiction to drugs, including alcohol. And religion has lifted people's eyes—however briefly—above the work they needed to do in order to eat and survive. As an interest, it has competed with money itself. Countless people have felt that without this influence their lives would have been more squalid.

Religion has been used by proud people as an excuse for their pride, but it is superficial to regard that as typical. Far more characteristic has been the humbling effect of a moral ideal. Religion has challenged people to be perfect, and has reminded them that, in comparison with the ideal, they have remained sinners. Those with some claim to be respectable or even righteous, and strong supporters of religion, have been described constantly as sinners. But religion has not remained content to denounce people. In many ways it has actively sought to help the sensitive, the anxious and the ashamed. It has disturbed the complacent, but it has also comforted the despondent. By rebukes and encouragements it has helped the production of the 'harvest of the Spirit' described by St Paul (a man who could be bitter, restless and conceited): 'love, joy, peace, patience, kindness, goodness, fidelity, gentleness and self-control'.

The fellowships known as Alcoholics Anonymous and Gamblers Anonymous consist of men, and some women, who have conquered the miseries of being compulsive alcoholics or compulsive gamblers, and who are helping others to do the same. They have a 'recovery programme' of twelve steps, which in simple terms sum up what religion has meant to millions of people.

1 We admitted we were powerless . . . that our lives had become unmanageable.
2 Came to believe that a Power greater than ourselves could restore us to a normal way of thinking and living.
3 Made a decision to turn our will and our lives over to the care of this Power (of our own understanding).
4 Made a searching and fearless moral and financial inventory of ourselves.
5 Admitted to ourselves and to another human being the exact nature of our wrongs.
6 Were entirely ready to have these defects of character removed.
7 Humbly asked God (of our understanding) to remove our shortcomings.
8 Made a list of all persons we had harmed and became willing to make amends to them all.
9 Made direct amends to such people wherever possible, except when to do so would injure them or others.
10 Continued to take personal inventory and, when

we were wrong, promptly admitted it.

11 Sought through prayer and meditation to improve our conscious contact with God as we understand him, praying only for knowledge of his will for us and the power to carry that out.

12 Having made an effort to practise these principles in all our affairs, we tried to carry this message to other compulsive alcoholics/gamblers.

Religion has sometimes been made a selfish emotion, but usually it has fought both the simple selfishness of greed or addiction and also the slightly broader selfishness which takes an interest in other people only when it is immediately convenient. Religion has bound together husband and wife in faithfulness through prosperity and adversity, and many families have found that religion has expressed, safeguarded and increased their unity. Religion has made neighbours come together to worship, to talk with each other and to help each other; in many places religious buildings have been the centres of community life. Religion has surrounded and blessed the patriotism of almost every nation, and in many cases religion has also embarrassed the nation, or the ruling group within a nation, by insisting that all men are brothers. If our respect for someone depends on how strong, handsome, intelligent or rich he or she is, obviously people are not equal. But if we value a person chiefly because he or she is capable of rising to the moral heights described by religion, then the great differences between individuals become relatively insignificant. A man struggles, and that gives him his dignity. It is true that the saint struggles more successfully than the average man, but the saint is more conscious than the average man that he is a sinner.

Tragically often religion has been a banner of a merely local pride instead of a stimulus to the universal. But most forms of religion have in them an inner tendency to the universal, because they offer an interpretation of the whole of the reality surrounding the worshipper. Worshippers come to acknowledge—however slowly—that if the religion contains truth, then this truth must be related to the whole of the reality it claims to describe. They have been forced by the pressure of religion to consider the world as well as the parish. Often, therefore, religion has meant more than an obsession with the local. It has taught the basic unity of mankind and the sacredness of Earth. Such teachings, if believed, are the strongest possible stimulus to seek understanding between nations and races and to enjoy Earth's riches in co-operation without gluttony. In the twentieth century many religious believers have derived such a vision of the world from their religious faith; examples are the successive Secretaries-General of the United Nations, the Christian Dag Hammarskjöld and the Buddhist U Thant.

One often finds in religion a tension between a concern for the world and a concern for the individual, who is believed to be in some sense immortal. The insistence on the supreme sacredness of each human life has, indeed, given rise to mistakes such as the religious opposition to birth control; from the excellent principle that each child is to be honoured some very influential religious teachers have drawn the very dangerous conclusion that the number of children born should not be limited artificially. But the crusade against contraception is being rapidly abandoned, and it seems clear that once this mistake has been disowned religion at its best could inspire the world order as it has inspired the neighbourhood and the nation—without losing sight of the individual's feelings and dreams. Religion can affirm the dignity of man against any ideology which would subordinate that dignity to an economic or political system; yet religion can also set the individual's dignity in the context of all life. For there is built into religion a reverence for nature, checking the impatience of man. There is also built into religion a reverence for those dead and those to come, checking the self-importance of the living. Everything and everyone are traced to the one divine source. Thus a religious reverence for life can inspire both a respect for the individual and a self-discipline.

And in religion, the belief in the basic unity of mankind has very often led into an insistence on the practical duty of personal charity to the stranger. It is tragically easy for people to use religion to strengthen their prejudices against those who are not immediately familiar or congenial, and it is tragically easy for the spokesmen of religion to gain local popularity by lending their authority to such evil. But there is a golden thread running through the history of religion: the nobility of compassion. Those parts of the religious scriptures which have taught compassion have been the parts enduring longest. Those holy and humble men and women who have shown compassion, making the unity of mankind immediate, have been the saints whose appeal has been deepest and widest.

2

Such is moral religion, and such is social religion—despite many features of the history of religion which help to persuade us to believe that, as religion teaches, man is sinful. But the most interesting part of religion lies elsewhere. At the heart of religion has been an experience far stronger than personal or social morality: mysticism.

As a word, 'mysticism' tends to put people off. It seems to suggest sentimentality, confusion of thought, and a sinister plot against science. Or it may suggest an unhealthy interest in a few hermits who have indulged in religious emotionalism instead of getting on with life. But authentic mysticism is no enemy of accurate, scientific thought. It is simply a different way of understanding life, useful for some purposes although not for all. In much the same way, getting to know a friend is neither better nor worse than the scientific study of psychology; it is different. And authentic mysticism is no enemy of a practical approach to life, any more than wanting to spend time with a friend means that one is lazy. Although one of the glories of the history of religion has been the intense, ecstatic experience recorded in fragments by the advanced mystics, anyone who prays has had an inkling of what the advanced mystics have struggled to express. This experience is a reality lying behind all the attempts to describe a supernatural 'other' world, but it is a reality which is important for our total understanding of ourselves and the world around us.

On the one hand, mysticism shows that people, or at least some people, have important capacities which are scarcely used in the everyday routine of life—or in intellectual work which is done by the analysing mind. In mysticism, a sense of wonder leads into a deeper understanding, and this leads into an indescribable joy. The ability to have that experience is the best thing about being human. On the other hand, mysticism shows—or seems to show—some truths about our surroundings: that they have a pattern, that this pattern makes sense to us, that it is beautiful to us, that it is something with which we can identify ourselves, that it is a pattern, a meaning, which gives us joy. Mysticism shows that we and our surroundings are more than natural if by the 'natural' we mean the trivial.

This strange but common experience can, it seems, be sparked off at almost any moment. People have had such feelings when seeing objects which are not usually thought of as at all remarkable, and when doing the most unromantic things. But naturally there have been many attempts to prepare for this experience, and to work out its results. The pleasure involved is so great that there has been an immense interest taken in the possibility of obtaining the experience through drugs—but ecstasy through dope can easily backfire ('the bad trip'). Even if the drugs do not poison the body or mind, their thrills are most unlikely to strengthen the whole personality as authentic mysticism does. Music and art are much safer roads into richer experience, but most people have found religion the best preparation for the desired vision and the best way of life to adopt after it. This is because religion, while it honours music and art very highly and uses them very extensively, is related to the whole personality in a way beyond music or art. Religion seeks to transform the daily routine, to glorify it, while the beauty of music or art often makes life seem more sordid than ever. Religion is an attempt to make the whole of human life dance in joy, in the light of the glory known in mystical experience.

With this purpose religion has become an educational system; and the pupils who have gone to learn from it, and who have not been disappointed, cannot be counted. But the main reason why religion has attracted this immense effort, and has rewarded it, has been that religion has raised the possibility that, in addition to ourselves and our surroundings, a third reality is experienced through mysticism: the reality of the divine. Many of the symbols used by religion are intended to help the exploration of this possibility that through mystical experience or humble prayer man encounters a divine presence in the midst of nature and history. This possibility has attracted and deeply moved many, from the simplest to the most learned. And the attraction is easy to understand once we have shaken off the silly prejudice which assumes the the divine must be boring.

The most learned man sees that, if the divine is a reality, then this must be *the* reality. In comparison with it all other things or people are unreal; and here must lie the clue to all the mystery that baffles us in nature and human history, although we are not capable of fully grasping the clue. The simplest person sees that this meeting with the divine can throw light on the darkness which surrounds the individual's life. Religion has been valued supremely in relation to birth and death. This has not meant merely supplying what the sociologists call 'the rites of passage'—the public ceremonies of the initiation (for example, the christening) and the funeral. It has meant what lies behind the ceremonies: a vision of the divine around the beginning and the end of each life. And between the beginning and the end, regular religious meditation has helped countless people to keep alive the vision of meaning.

Any person's life, with or without belief in the divine, can have a certain amount of meaning. Sexual love, the bringing up of a family, growth in emotional stature through friendship—these all bring meaning. Many people find meaning in their work, even in our industrial society. Many find it through many loyalties. The search for truth through education and research is one activity which carries its own meaning. The appreciation of beauty is another, more common. Happy lives can be crowded with such meanings. But the meaning given to life by belief in the divine is greater because belief in the divine is held to put one in touch with the source and goal of all that is, and to assure one that one's own life is held securely in this framework of meaning. Even lives which are comparatively empty of the other meanings, or where the other meanings are fading away at the approach of death, are given this ultimate meaning—while for happy people brimming over with an active life all the other meanings form introductions to this glory which begins, supports and fulfils them all. It is understandable why some religious people, concentrating their hopes on this ultimate meaning, make the mistake of thinking that life for non-believers must be completely meaningless. For belief in the divine makes life a journey with a destination. All love, for example, is regarded as a training to love and enjoy the divine. All loyalty leads into worship, and all the restlessness in the human spirit is an appetite for the perfect beauty which is completely true.

The existence of this appetite does not guarantee its satisfaction, any more than the existence of a thirst guarantees the possibility of a drink. In this chapter we are considering only the human value of religion, not its ultimate truth. Here it will be enough to state that the religious development of man has greatly stretched his capacities. If we were to agree that there is no divine reality outside man's imagination, we should still have to contradict the suggestion that religion is always a kind of mental sickness. We should also have to deny that all religion can easily be ridiculed as the product of human weakness. Although religion has often been trivial, and has been corrupted in many evil ways, real religion is the highest possible form of spiritual wisdom. It is rare because it is difficult. It demands that many interests should all be held together because they are all parts of the one quest for the divine reality.

In serious religion the greatest interest is taken in the possibility of personally meeting the divine—but never so as to forget the concerns of moral religion or social religion. Our encounter with the divine is thought of as a gift which comes surprisingly and which we cannot earn—but which we should try our utmost to deserve by self-discipline. It is treated as eerie and baffling—but always the attempt is made to think about it as strenuously as possible. Religion is known to be in essence an affair of the heart, deeply emotional and 'subjective'—but a thorough effort is made to relate it to the 'objective' world around us. Religion is in its inner life always fresh because the experience on which it rests is always contemporary—but no light which the past can throw is neglected.

The awareness of the divine presence, when this is more than a superficial or second-hand awareness, is frightened, but fascinated. It is awestruck, but it gives rise to the most intense joy known to man. It is silent, but it inspires endless celebration and reflection. It produces thankfulness, but never complacency; confidence, but never laziness. It results in dependence on the divine, but also in a new energy and strength. It produces a childlike attitude of trusting acceptance, but those most experienced in communion with the divine have often been regarded by their contemporaries and by subsequent generations as the most mature human beings. And the characteristics which we have been describing have been observed in people with or without special gifts of mystical insight, wherever prayer has been practised. These are the marks of holiness to be found in all the saints. But they also mark men of the world such as Alcoholics Anonymous and Gamblers Anonymous, as these men turn in their need to 'a Power greater than ourselves'.

3

We are being true to the facts if we conclude that religion has on the whole had a psychologically beneficial influence on mankind, despite all the evils to be seen in the history of religion. But we have agreed that there must be an element of faith in the interpretation of the mystical experience on which religion is based. This faith is not merely faith in the particular images through which the mystical experience is expressed. Such images can be admitted to be imaginary—and still the basic belief is not touched, for the basic belief is that the experience is about a reality greater than any image of it. It is true to say that religion is kept going by belief. To many, this seems an argument against religion, for two reasons.

The first reason is that belief is not proof. This is true, and religious believers should continually remind themselves of this truth when tempted to claim a certainty to which they are not entitled and which they do not feel in their hearts unless they are too ignorant or stupid to reckon with the evidence counting against belief. But many valuable activities in life depend on belief, not on proof. Science does, up to a point; for a creative scientist has a 'hunch' before any experiment can test his theory. Above all, personal and social morality depends on belief in some values which cannot be tested as the commercial value of a commodity can be. Patriotism, for example, depends on an emotional attitude to a country, a basic acceptance of it, and a commitment to its service. Above all, friendship and love depend on belief in the merits and attractiveness of other people. A citizen of another country, or the lover of another girl, cannot be forced to share one's belief by intellectual proof. In fact, onlookers frequently comment, 'I can't see what he sees in her'. Nobody leads a creative life without being willing to act on faith. Indeed, in life what we feel we must believe is always more important than what we can prove. We need faith as we need food.

The second reason urged against religious belief is that it is too good to be true. The willingness to believe in a scientific theory, or in a political cause, or in a person, is regarded as valuable by everyone who has thought about life. But religious belief is much broader. It is an acceptance of life as a whole as good, and it is a commitment of all one's powers—emotional, mental and practical; heart, mind and strength—in response to this goodness. That attitude certainly goes beyond what can be proved about life, and it may seem to go beyond what can reasonably be said about it. In particular, many modern people feel that the divine may be no more than the memory of a parent loved or feared in childhood. However, before yielding to this objection we need to remember how often in our daily experience we meet situations where we could take either a constructive or a defeatist view; and how often we take the attitude of optimism instinctively and find that it leads to solid success. Analysed intellectually the evidence before us could suggest either a positive or a negative conclusion, but we decide to be positive. The cheerfulness of religious belief is only applying to life as a whole an attitude which we value in many practical problems. Certainly religion uses memories of childhood, but that need not discredit religion's verdict on grown-up life—any more than the rejection of religion need be attributed solely to an infantile rejection of parental love. It is true that religious belief has often led to religious credulity; too many things have been believed. But the remedy against this is not to insist on proof in the field of religion—the remedy is to be much clearer about what religion can teach us and what it cannot. The remedy is not to say that what is depressing must be what is most real—the remedy is to be much clearer about what is the joy which religion alone brings. Religious belief does not mean believing in statements which are contradicted by the evidence: it does not mean that today is going to be fine when in fact the rain is pouring down steadily. Religious belief is, in fact, much more like believing in a person than it is like believing that such-and-such is the case. To be sure, when we 'believe *in* a person' we believe certain things about that person—that he or she is alive, that he or she has certain characteristics, that his or her character will lead to certain actions in the future. But religious belief is much more like commitment to a person in love than it is like commitment to a theory.

So far, however, we have deliberately discussed 'religion', rather than belief in God exclusively. This is because the value of religion is not confined to the tradition which regards the divine as single or personal. The founder of Buddhism, for example, refused to teach about the possible existence of God or gods.[1] There have been other forms of religion involving worship but not the worship of any God believed to transcend the things and people around. For example, many have worshipped nature as divine (pantheism). Only one conclusion does justice to the evidence: moral, social and mystical religion develops the humanity of man as a spiritual being before it goes down on its knees before God.

But we may now consider the validity of belief in God.

[1] But in practice Buddhism has often embraced, or come close to, belief in God. The goal of *nirvana* (Nothingness)—originally the one escape from the endless cycle of reincarnation—has been presented positively, as the glory greater than all things, and many figures in Buddhism, including the Buddha himself, have been treated as divine.

V

GOD: CREDIBLE?

I

Belief in God is a form of religion which affirms that the divine reality is single and personal. That affirmation is essentially very simple. It does not necessarily involve elaborate descriptions of the supernatural 'other' world. On the contrary, it rejects and fights any tendency to make the many imagined inhabitants of that 'other' world divine or semi-divine. Why, then, does it *not* treat God as a creature of man's imagination? It certainly does regard all pictures of God as man-made. Why is God himself thought to be real, and more real than oneself? Why is he thought to be more real than anything or anyone else one can know or conceive? Such belief springs out of one's experience. It need not involve the acceptance of any dogma not corresponding with one's own experience.

One believes in God because his reality has been disclosed to one, although the disclosure in one's own experience may have been very tantalizing. Of course we do not have to rely entirely on our own experience—any more than, when we accept science, we rely on our own scientific experiments. We usually acquire belief in God, if we acquire it at all, from parents, school teachers and religious leaders. We accept what they tell us about religion, as we accept what the scientific text-books tell us. But still experience lies behind. Behind the text-books lie scientific experiments which have been made, and behind the religious teaching which we accept lies religious experience. If we do not think that our parents or teachers have found their teaching to be true in their own experience, we reject it; a family or a school or a church where the religion is hollow is a family or a school or a church where the religion is fruitless. And we know that we can, at least to some extent, conduct our own experiments to verify what has been told us, in religion as in science. Belief in God can become real to us through our own reflection on our own lives. Indeed, it must become real in that way if it is to be mature. And since we can say very little about God as he is in himself, the significance of God-talk depends on whether we have experienced God as he is in relation to us. Only if we have reason to believe that God has disclosed himself to us does our talk about him have meaning.

The moments of God's self-disclosure are parts of the 'mystical' experience. They are moments of understanding ourselves and our surroundings as one pattern of meaning, beauty and joy. But the person who believes in God draws a special meaning out of this common experience. The process of drawing out this special meaning should not be regarded as obviously unreal or unreasonable; countless people with mystical experience have felt that it was reasonable to interpret the reality in this way. The special meaning has two main features, already indicated by saying that to call the divine reality 'God' is to say that the divine reality is *single* and *personal.*

Usually when we interpret any experience we try to see the underlying connections between one part and another. To believe in God is to believe that there is a unity underlying all that exists, because everything and everyone has a single divine source. No one can prove it. It may be too good to be true. But it is the supreme example of the attempt of man's mind to find order where, at first sight, there seems to be chaos. Science, art and many everyday activities are other examples of the drive to a single explanation. Most of us have a drive in us which makes us tidy up a room—or a jumble of evidence. Belief in God is the conviction that this drive enables a discovery in the field explored by mystical experience or prayer.

Some of the most powerful expressions of this belief in the One are in the Hindu sacred books, but all real belief in God, however it is expressed, affirms the ultimate unity —it may be, after many hesitations. This is not to say that everyone believes 'deep down' in God. Some theologians have claimed that, because to them the unity underlying all that exists is the basis on which they think and live, everyone else must in his heart of hearts think the same. Some theologians have tried to argue with sceptics: you already agree that 'Being' underlies all existence, you ought to go on to agree that this 'Being' is best described in the Christians' talk of 'God'. But the sceptics are not convinced, because the preliminary talk about 'Being' does not appeal to them. They have not vividly experienced the unity underlying all that exists. They regard existence as 'one thing after another'. The mysticism in the talk about 'Being' seems to them nonsense. Believers in God ought to sympathize with the difficulty sceptics have in seeing this underlying unity, for the believers ought to be the first to say that they would not have seen it without God's self-disclosure. And they ought to be the first to admit that the history of religion shows how difficult it is to be a thorough believer in the divine reality as a single reality.

Various tests show whether our belief in this ultimate unity is genuine. Does our religion describe the divine reality in a complicated way, for example by telling many stories about many gods who are equally divine (polytheism)? If the many pictures of the divine are treated as being of equal value, then our religion has not got beyond the pictures to the ultimate reality; it is still playing around. Or perhaps our religion is seriously confused. Do we allow ourselves to be fascinated and controlled by powers which are not subordinated to the God we vaguely 'believe in'? Whatever our theoretical values may be, in practice do we treat sex, money or the State as what matters supremely? Many Westerners in the twentieth century—people who would ignorantly reject any identification with primitive peasants who have many gods—appear to have indulged in such worship. And many in East and West with minds above all this superstition and sensuality have still found themselves unable to regard the ultimate reality as single. Instead they have thought of life as a struggle between equally strong forces of progress and disaster, order and disorder, light and darkness. And many who believe that they believe in one God find conflicting characteristics in him—saying, for example, that he is both beautiful and ugly, both loving and cruel, both attractive and terrifying. This may be a recognition that no single word can cover the total reality, and thus a healthy recognition of the mystery always surrounding God; but the confusion in men's speech may also show that they have not yet thought out what is God's character. And many find God in one sector of life while other sectors are left outside their faith. For example, does our religion find that God is real in the countryside, while the city is Godless? Or is it near to God on Sunday, but not on Monday? If so, such hesitation may be an honest way of acknowledging the limitations of man's ability to understand God—but it may also show that we are unable to believe that the divine reality is single. To believe this means to believe that there is a reality more real than the pictures and puzzles which otherwise keep the interpretation of our experience in fragments. He is not many gods. He does not have many characters. He does not cease to be real at any point.

This God is called 'he' because the one divine reality

must be personal or more than personal.

It is true that calling God personal can result in many errors. Some of these errors are simply childish ones; God is treated as no more than an invisible father. Or a portrait of him can be treated as if it were an accurate photograph, and his character can be discussed as if he were a man. Such errors result from trivial attitudes to the divine reality, and make many puzzles about God insoluble. And thinking that God is a person as we are people can mean forgetting that, if he is real, he is not a person separate from us but is the source of *all* personality, deep in us. God includes all individuals. These are among the reasons why religious reformers in many times and places have had to warn believers in God against the worship of idols, including the idol of God pictured naïvely as a man.

But if God is really the source of all that exists he cannot be *less* than personal, because we are personal and he who is our source cannot be our inferior. In practice, regarding God as impersonal has often meant treating the divine reality as less significant than a person—for example, as less important than one's husband or wife. The impersonal God, the divine It, is kept in the background of philosophical speculation. Or what is worse: the word 'God' may simply become a label pinned on the best part of the one person who really does interest me, myself. Only if the personality in God as 'the Other' is acknowledged does it become possible to begin with him the personal relationship of frequent prayer. During the course of this relationship, one gradually begins to see how one ought to change and to work in response; in other words, one begins to know God's will. And one gradually begins to understand why the growing loyalty in this relationship has so often been compared with human marriage.

Such talk about God can easily become sentimental. But the actual experience is no more sentimental than a strong marriage. It is deeply emotional, but it involves one's will in relation to another's—and it is severely practical, for it means changing one's selfish habits in order to live with someone else. To make this clearer, the comparison between life with God and the married life should be joined by another comparison, also constantly repeated when men have thought about God. This is the comparison between God and a judge. Most of us come to marriage by falling in love. But few of us come to the personal God by loving him. On the contrary, we come to him because in the pattern which life begins to take for us we feel the pressure of his personality far more unpleasantly. Although the basic religious sense was cheerful, this further experience of the divine reality is disturbing. We feel the challenge of his will against our greed and selfishness, and against the follies of our world. We grow convinced that disaster will come if his will is not obeyed, and we compare this with a sentence by a judge. Step by step we are driven into doing his will. We enter the love of God by the fear of God. It is only gradually that we learn that God is more like a lover than like a judge, for it is only gradually that we learn that what appeared to us as his anger was in fact the tough side of love, demanding the best. In our experience of the real God, there is no room for sentimentality—or triviality.

A more basic criticism of belief in God also deserves consideration. Is the personal God entirely created by man's own imagination? To believers in God who have begun to obey him, the personality they glimpse behind their total experience becomes fascinating, and the love which is now possible is their chief duty and delight. W. H. Auden summed up a vast tradition of devotion in his already famous lines:

Space is the Whom our loves are needed by,
Time is our choice of How to love and Why.

But such poetry needs explaining if it is not to be treated as just another example of the tendency in old-fashioned poetry to address sentimental compliments to lifeless objects which cannot in fact hear them. Is Auden here like a poet talking to a tree? Or is he like a drunk, talking to a lamp-post or to an imaginary pink rabbit?

Of course there is a poetic, symbolic or imaginary, element in every attempt to describe or picture God. But the basic question is whether it is better to compare the ultimate reality with a thing or with a person. Much of human life is occupied by dealing with things, and usually the only sensible course is to deal with things as they are, unemotionally, and to use them. Objects ought to be looked at objectively, and many of them ought to be pushed around. Driving a car is an obvious example. But if our reactions to our environment are to be fully human, we must sometimes lift our eyes above this level, and react to our environment as a whole with wonder. And at this level of understanding life as literally marvellous, the reactions which we have developed when dealing with things may not be the most useful.

We can only understand a very little about our environment as a whole, or about the meaning of life for us. But if we patiently watch this phenomenon and live with it, we find that we slowly observe certain characteristics in it. We find also that the best way of understanding these characteristics is to use the experience we have gained in dealing with people, not things. Understanding life in its spiritual reality is not really like driving a car, or sitting on a chair. It is much more like sitting on a cat—and it is even more like sitting on a friend by accident. At point after point, our experience of people can provide a clue. For living people can never be understood completely.

Even the person one is married to remains a mystery to the end. And people cannot be looked at unemotionally if one really wants to meet them. One must be prepared to open up oneself, and to involve oneself. And people cannot be manipulated without any regard to their feelings; if one pushes them around, they push back, except in rare situations where they are so afraid that they wish to obey. To understand people, we have to watch their actions. One can understand a table by inspecting it, if necessary through a microscope, or by carving it up. One cannot understand a person sitting at a table except by waiting for that person's character to unfold in conversation and behaviour. To understand this marvellous life, we have to be humble and patient, for we are 'face to face' with a great mystery. It is (we may conclude) useful to talk about it in personal terms, while all the time remembering that this mystery is really more than a person. Of course it is true that the use of personal terms can be a mark of childishness, as when a young child talks to a toy. But it need not follow that this kind of understanding of life is always and merely childish. On the contrary, much experience of personal relations, and much wisdom, may be essential before one is mature enough to reach this understanding.

To believe in God is to keep all our powers of dealing with things as they are, one by one, but to add a new power of responding to our environment as a whole. If we are wise, we shall respond to the marvel of life by treating the reality behind it as personal or more than personal. Although all pictures of this reality are based partly on our own imaginations, we find it more useful to make pictures based partly on our experience of *people* than to have no pictures at all, or to have pictures based only on our experience of things. What, then, is the difference between the kind of attitude which a carpenter or poet has when he treats a piece of wood or a tree with respect, almost as if it were alive, and the response which the believer in God makes by fearing and loving the 'Whom' in and behind Space? It is the difference made by believing in God as Creator.

2

The creation of all that exists by God has often been pictured as an action long ago complete, like the making of something by a craftsman. That is the picture given in many of the world's sacred books, including Genesis in the Old Testament. It is a mythological picture, and it can be seriously misleading.

As an account of the origins of the universe, Earth and life, this picture seems to be a rival account to science's. Great damage has been done when believers in God have felt themselves obliged to defend it against scientific inquiry. But the truth is that the mythological picture provides no information whatever about the detailed origins. Anything we can know about these, we can know from science. Belief in God the Creator goes back behind the detailed origins—that is, behind the stage where the scientist begins. It goes back behind the 'big bang' which produced the primordial particles some 20,000 million years ago—and behind whatever other scientific account of the origins of the universe may seem better. Science takes certain things for granted. To it, the universe simply has certain potentialities, and everything follows from that. Belief in God tries to penetrate the mystery of who granted these things, or why the universe has these potentialities. But belief can never return from its exploration of this mystery of the 'Final Cause' with anything resembling scientific knowledge.

Speculation about the 'Final Cause' has, in fact, never

got anyone anywhere, and in the modern world fewer people than ever before are interested in it. More relevant is the fact that the mythological accounts of the creation have seemed to be rivals to the scientific account of the evolution of *Homo sapiens* from other animals. Much time has been wasted on this rivalry between Genesis and science. But the truth is that if we want to know *how* mankind arose, we must turn to science. It is the question *why* that concerns religion. Belief in God tries to understand the purpose behind the creation of matter, the emergence of life from matter, and the evolution of man—of course, from the standpoint provided by the evolution of man. This can all be analysed as chance, and chance—or, rather, a prodigious waste which must seem to us to resemble chance—certainly plays a major role in it all. The process culminating in the evolution of man appears, however, to have a pattern, despite much waste; and that pattern, despite many obscurities, appears to make for progress, despite many setbacks. Many scientists of great knowledge and integrity have thought so. Belief in God the Creator sees, as this lies hidden in the origins, the purpose which can be seen a little more clearly when the progress has emerged. It is like viewing the bits of a puzzle when one knows how the puzzle is solved. Or it is like climbing a mountain and looking down on the route one took.

It may be that if one concentrates one's attention on the end-product one can glimpse some point even in the apparent waste in nature. The science of genetics may provide an example. The genes which carry instructions for the physical foundations of the lives of new people and other organisms are, from the point of view of the biochemist, threads of nucleic acids. When, due to some chemical reaction or to radiation, an acid has a 'fault' in it as it carries the instructions for a new life, a genetic mutation occurs. These mutations are unrelated to the organism's needs. Most mutations do damage, but when a mutation adapts an animal or other organism to cope better with its environment—or to cope better with changes in the environment happening long after the mutation—progress occurs, because the less fortunate animals or organisms whose genes have not changed cannot stand the struggle and they die out. That certainly seems a highly odd way of introducing novelty and progress. It is not surprising that no one understood it before the twentieth century. Not one of us, if asked to play the Creator, would set about the business by arranging for the natural selection of mutant genes. But the fact that it seems to us odd is not a good argument for saying that it is impossible. Even if there is no Creator, everyone must be astounded by the whole business of storing up the genetic instructions for a complete, adult, human body in one egg, in size one tenth of the diameter of a pinhead, fertilized in the female by one very much smaller sperm among millions racing to that egg from the male. It seems such an impossible start to a human life—yet it happens. And it may be that this odd way of creating new life is the *only* way of introducing novelty without the dictatorial control or the miraculous intervention which the Creator has rejected; as a method, it respects both the freedom and the order in the natural processes. And it may be claimed that this method works well on the whole. It may be that the Creator's chosen method is justified by the tendency of its results—as one can see when one looks back. At least we should recall that nature, despite its colossal 'waste', has scored successes on such a scale that many generations of intelligent people thought that every detail in it had been ordered by God's miraculous care in a purposive design.

But God's purpose in nature can never be seen very

clearly (as we have already admitted). The real interest to us of the belief that God is Creator has not so far been mentioned. If the divine reality which we call God is the source of everything and everyone, the most important truth for us to realize must be that he is the cause of everything and everyone, including ourselves, *now*. The claim behind the mythological pictures is the claim that all that exists, or is possible, is dependent on this one ultimate and necessary source. If the claim is true, the dependence on the 'Ground of Being' began when things and life began—but what matters to us is that both we and our surroundings are dependent: that we are not completely the products of blind chance, and that our surroundings are not. And the historical investigation of many creation myths in the world's scriptures has shown that they actually arose out of an experienced crisis, not out of speculation about origins. For example, the first chapter of Genesis arose out of the Jews' experience of exile in Babylon. Confronted by the temples of their conquerors and by the prosperous cities around them, the Jews asked themselves in despair whether the God they worshipped, 'Yahweh', was the Lord and therefore the Creator of the whole world. In order to express their final faith that he was, they took the Babylonian myths about the creation and defiantly edited them to show the supremacy of Yahweh.

Belief in God the Creator is therefore chiefly the result of personal experience of dependence on God. What really interests me is not the Final Cause, but the cause of me. Because we think that we depend on this source, we try to work out how everything and everyone depend. Without this personal experience, the general belief would be futile speculation, like the general theory of music to a person who is tone-deaf.

The mythological picture of the Creator as the master-craftsman 'in the beginning' can also mislead through its comparisons between God and the craftsman, and between the universe and the craftsman's material. The man is given it, stands over it, and works on it. But nothing can be given to God as raw material. Whatever exists must come from the one source of God's own Being. And God cannot be separated from anything that exists. Since he is its source and its continuous creator, it would collapse into non-existence if his presence were withdrawn, as the print on this page would disappear if the paper were burned. Therefore God must be constantly thought of as being everywhere. The mythological picture of God the master-craftsman has had disastrous consequences by suggesting that he is separate from his creation. This picture was inspired by reverence for the supremacy of God over his creation, but in practice it has often resulted in thinking of God as remote from it. Belief in God the Creator means thinking of all that exists as being alive with some of his life; and, what matters most to me, it means thinking of him as alive in me.

The enduring value of the myth of the Master-Craftsman lies in its suggestion that the divine reality is not exhausted by the creation. Even a master-craftsman who 'puts all that he has' into his work remains greater than that work. Belief in God the Creator refuses to separate him from his creation, but it also refuses to identify him entirely with it. There is more beyond. In that sense—and in that sense only—God is supernatural. This is believed because of another experience, to which we now turn.

3

It is the experience of seeing how unsatisfactory the creation is at present. If the universe around us all appealed to us equally, we could worship it as divine. But in fact the universe is *not* equally adorable. Some of it acutely offends our sense of morality, which is the reason why the 'problem of evil' so often arises in our minds to question belief in a good purpose behind all that exists. Experience shows that it is as difficult to worship the whole lot as it is to be in love with a crowd. It is indeed possible to abandon belief in God because of this, arguing as so many have argued that a good God could not have been responsible for a creation containing so much evil. On the other hand, it is possible to refine belief in God in the fires of this problem, if one refuses to let go of the good in the creation—the good which suggested this belief in the first place.

At its most basic level, belief in the divine reality arises out of wonder that anything should exist rather than nothing. Most believers have felt this wonder vividly for themselves, although people can take the fact of existence for granted. To believe in the divine is to marvel like a tourist in front of the fountain of 'Being' which endlessly cascades into existence. But what gives this basic belief its growing character is its increasing conviction that the good in existence matters more than the evil. This conviction is, of course, a matter of choice. It is possible to emphasize the evil, to see the universe as a mere mess or even as a place of torture, and to conclude often that suicide is the only wisdom. Most people, however, make another choice. They choose to walk by their moments of light rather than to be sucked into the darkness. At its most intense, this choice comes in the joyous interpretation of the mystical experience, as the assurance that basically all is well. People who make that choice feel less like tourists admiring a fountain and more like children jumping into it on a blazing hot day, swimming, splashing and shouting in fun. To many all that they see of good is summed up when they call the divine reality

'God'. But as they begin to experience this God, and struggle to think about him, they grow convinced that, if he is better than the creation as a whole is, yet is felt to be more than a mere portion of it, a result must follow. He must be worshipped as the one reality greater than the creation itself. He is beyond the existence which has its source in him. He is not confined by Space; he is more, he is infinite. He is not confined by Time; he is more, he is eternal.

As we realize how unsatisfactory the creation is, we ask that it should be put right. We ask that what now seems pointless should be brought more fully into the purpose we have glimpsed, that what now seems ugly should be brought into the beauty we know, and above all that what offends our moral sense should be subordinated to a good purpose. To put it in terms of belief in a personal God, we ask that the Creator should rule more clearly; we want a stronger government. To believe in God is to trust that this development for which we ask is beginning to take place. Very seldom do we see it as clearly as we should like, but we believe in God because we think that we have begun to see it from time to time.

It is a development which, we observe, is slow to solve the problems and astonishingly gentle in overcoming obstacles. For long periods there seems to be no development at all. When progress does come, it occurs as part of a spurt of energy which also has many effects which do not turn out to be progressive. Any opposition to the progress seems enough to defeat it except in rare instances; yet on those instances development depends. And all this takes vast tracts of time. Such is the pattern which scientists observe in evolution, and the same pattern is experienced by us in the growth of our own gardens and of our own children, and in the development of our own affairs: in what is grandly called 'cultural evolution'. Of course we grow impatient. But we find that only one explanation is possible—if we believe in God. It is the explanation that the power exercised by God over his creation is never dictatorial power. The words 'Almighty' and 'Omnipotent', when used about God, may easily mislead. We observe that God's power is limited by the reality of his creation. Because of the reverence for him which we have learned from our experience, we conclude that it is limited by his own choice, but limited it is. His method, as we see it in action, resembles persuasion rather than coercion. He behaves more like a worker than like a monarch. And he does not run; slowly, he seems to grope his way forward.

We ask ourselves why such a patience should be the chosen method of developing an unsatisfactory creation. We never find the complete answer to that question, for the divine patience allows great disasters and sufferings which we cannot justify even when we know what progress occurs. But part of the answer comes to us in the faith that the real God, who is so amazingly patient, has in all this a motive not unlike the patient love of a parent for a child. We ask ourselves why this God, if he is real, so often hides himself. We never find the complete answer to that question either, for the divine modesty allows some earnest people to undergo agonized years of seeking without finding—when we, if we had the power, would show ourselves. But part of the answer that we do see is that the real God is more interested in how we develop by coping with our uncertainty than he is interested in how accurately we understand and describe his method. The only clue to these mysteries seems to be provided by thinking of God's love as limiting his power, in much the same way as a parent's ability to push a child around is in practice limited by his or her affection. This is a wise way of working only if God's purpose is much the same as a parent's. The parent hopes that if the child's freedom is respected the child will in the end be stronger. God hopes that the final glory will be greater after the working out of the method he has chosen.

Such a choice only makes sense if the result is supremely important to God, in much the same way as a child's success is supremely important to a parent. The disorder and suffering involved in the creation cannot be justified except with reference to the end. Somehow the successful completion of his work according to his method must enrich God and add to the divine reality. Somehow God's perfection is not static, but can be improved by the completion. Somehow events have consequences for God. Great religious teachers seem to have had this in mind when they have constantly emphasized the joy of God—a joy already great beyond man's understanding but increasing as God's purpose reaches triumph. They have also spoken freely of the sorrow of God—a sorrow greater than ours, and endured until that triumph.

That is an austere vision of God. It has to be, if it is to be true to the facts of God's creation. Belief in God means wrestling with a mystery, and it means confessing that the God who is gradually experienced as real is not the God we probably wanted to meet; we should have preferred a God who used his power in order to make life perfect for us immediately. But because there is no room left for sentimentality in our belief in the real God, this belief is in touch with reality. And any disappointment involved can be blotted out by another experience which we can have.

This is the experience of a mysticism which is felt to be not only an introduction to God but also a union with God. It is the experience of identifying oneself with the purpose of God in his creation. This again is a painful experience, because the pains of the creation overwhelm one. But the person who enters into communion with God finds a deep understanding of God's steady purpose and an entry into God's growing joy. The result is that one surrenders bit by bit to the 'Whom' in Space, to the Creator of Space; and all the time one has seems too short for the conversation. And the most useful pictures of this overwhelming reality do seem to be those derived from intimately personal experiences. For the best comparisons are between the worship of God and a young child's relationship with loving parents; and between union with God and the sexual intercourse of those who are committed to each other entirely in marriage. Like the other forms of mysticism, this mysticism of union with God has produced many records of outstanding spiritual quality. But just as the other forms of mysticism are not the monopoly of the experts, so some taste of the meaning here has come to all who pray to God—and to many others, including many of those who have abandoned formal prayer because they have identified it with dangerous illusions about the supernatural 'other' world. The great novelist Albert Camus, who profoundly analysed the sickness and the hope of the modern spirit, once wrote, 'Secret of my universe: imagine God without the immortality of the soul.'

4

So far we have discussed the general, human belief in God, not any specific form of that belief belonging to a particular religious tradition. This is because belief in God is far wider than, say, Christianity is, and can be presented and analysed on the basis of common human experience. But very few people rest content with the position we have reached so far. Most people find that they must turn to a particular religious tradition. This is because it is not strong enough to say that religion is valuable and that, as an interpretation of religion, the idea of God is credible. This position is too abstract, too vague. Almost everyone who has become interested in the divine reality eagerly wants to know more than this. The question arises: in real history, has God been seen, or at least glimpsed, more fully?

VI

GOD: GLIMPSED?

I

People have been aware of the divine, and have believed in God, in circumstances and for reasons which have been too varied to be described in even the longest of books. In the twentieth century, as the traditional Christian account of the supernatural 'other' world has lost credibility, many people in countries which had been dominated by Christianity have turned to the religions of Africa and Asia in order to get some fresh understanding of the divine, and they have not been disappointed. African dancing, which is a religious activity, has, through the Christianized American Negroes, influenced music all over the West; and through this, it has brought people together and made them forget their anxieties. That is only one example of black being beautiful to emotionally underdeveloped white Americans and Europeans. We have only to think of the prestige of Gandhi, or of the appeal of Hindu or Buddhist philosophy to inquiring spirits, or of the special attractiveness of the Zen cult, to realize the debt of the West to the East.

The needs expressed in spiritual movements in the West outside the churches and theology show clearly enough why the ancient wisdom of Africa and the East has had this modern influence. Many Westerners have grown inwardly weary of the constant rush and noise, and have begun to learn afresh the happiness of being still in silence. They have grown bored with a life measured by commercial success, and have been intrigued by the very different values which are still powerful in, for example, India. Eastern teachers have been listened to when they have defined success in terms of maturity rather than money, and when, instead of urging the conquest and exploitation of everything in sight, they have recommended a humble absorption into the divine which is everywhere around everyone. Instead of the logic of the West, the reliance on intuition has seemed the best guide to life, and instead of the loneliness of the West, the community spirit surviving in an unfragmented society has seemed the great source of human happiness. All this has supplied the West with some of the spiritual food which it has needed in its religious famine, and which it has been unable or unwilling to find in its own religious tradition.

However, more than this is needed. A definite attitude to modernization is needed in countries which, for better or for worse, have been modernized. In such countries, unless religion has something positive to say about the development of the modern world, it will remain on the fringe of that world and constantly exposed to defeat by it. Religion will be romantic rather than vital. It will be an interest, even a curiosity, of those who do not have to meet the pressures of modern life; it will not be the power behind those who have to master these pressures. It will appeal to young rebels, not to people at work; to the retired, not to the active. It will be a subject to enrich one's recreation, not the force inspiring daily life—or it will be the escapism of the defeated and despairing. The problem here is that the great, historic religions of Asia and Africa acquired their characters long before those continents were subjected to the pressures and opportunities of modernity. In Asia and Africa ways are being found of modernizing traditional religion, but it is a fact that this modernization of religion, so that it welcomes change and affirms life, owes much to the contact with the religion exported from the West. Within the West, the problems of modernizing the Western religious tradition have often been stressed—for example, in this book. But Western religion has been involved more closely with the forces which have made the modern world. Indeed, it gave birth to some of those forces. Those who seek a religious future for the West would surely be sensible to look again at the West's own religious roots.[1]

When examined, the Western religious tradition turns out to include the elements which in our own time have been found missing in the West and have therefore been imported from Asia and Africa. But it includes other elements, too, going back to another source, admittedly not European or American. We can adopt shock tactics, and can at once name this source: *the prophets of ancient Israel.*

It is easy for people today to laugh at the mere mention of this dead society, but people who are educated enough to know about the influence of ancient Israel do not find the subject ludicrous. The religion of ancient Israel, which its prophets influenced so greatly, was essential to the birth of Judaism, Christianity and Islam. It was also the source of important values held by modern people who do not adhere to any of those religions. In these ways ancient Israel wields a power more impressive than the military power of the modern state of Israel. It is also easy for modern people to be amused by a prophet's claim to foretell the future. But these men based any power of prediction which they may have possessed on a far more important capacity to see what was already going on. A racing tipster derives his guesses from his knowledge of how the horses have already run—but these men prophesied after watching nations and empires. They could,

[1] I attempted a rather longer assessment of 'light from the East' in my *Religion and Change* (Hodder and Stoughton, 1969).

and did, make mistakes about the future. Some of their threats and some of their promises were falsified by events. But they were still honoured if they had helped their contemporaries to glimpse the basic pattern in events. And serious people have this in mind when they say that our time needs prophets. That is why the literature known as 'futurology' has flourished in recent years, although we all know that even tomorrow's weather cannot always be forecast accurately.

In the religious crisis of the modern world, it is worth turning to these strange prophets with our modern questions.

2

Many of their themes authenticate themselves rapidly in our own crisis. Take the theme of humanity versus so-called 'progress'. The prophets of ancient Israel spoke up for the little man. In theory, and to some extent in practice, the old days had given to each Israelite his own place where he could feed his own family by his own work. Seven or eight hundred years before Christ there was a new economic growth-rate; and, with the affluence, a new exploitation. That was the landscape of the thunder of Elijah, Amos and Micah. Running through all the valid prophecy in the modern world there has been the insistence that technical advances must be subordinated to the needs of humanity. *People matter*—one by one, each with his or her own dignity, which must not be sacrificed to the multiplication of wealth in the hands of the few or to the idol of technology. Those who are untrained, or chronically sick, or tied to the home, or nailed to a fixed income, or not fortunate enough to be a native of a rich country—they matter. Any development is to be judged by the criterion of their progress.

Or take the theme of humanity versus so-called 'patriotism'. Amos made it disturbingly clear that he viewed Israel and Judah on the same level as Damascus, Gaza, Tyre, Edom, Ammon and Moab—countries well known in Israel and Judah as being foreign and wicked. And the unknown, exiled prophet called 'Second Isaiah' (Isaiah 40-55) viewed all nations in a common destiny of glory; this planet was seen as one from a ghetto in Babylon twenty-five centuries before it was seen from the moon. Essentially the same consciousness of the world's single tragedy and hope has been the undercurrent of true prophecy beneath all the fanatical and brutal nationalisms and racisms of our time. We therefore take it for granted that every true prophet will in a fresh way repeat the world-embracing theme of our common humanity. He will repeat, too, the other theme of the supremacy of the human within each society in the world.

However, there is more in the legacy of ancient Israel's prophets. The social injustice and national arrogance of Israel interested these men chiefly because Israel was, they said, the people of God; chosen first by God's favour, but then, because of these sins, singled out in God's anger. Of course the men who asserted that God was among Israel's enemies were without honour in their own time and country. We may gain some understanding of their courage if we contemplate what an outcry would surround any Jew who dared to say that the calamities of Jewry in the twentieth century were a just punishment of Jewish arrogance—and that the modern state of Israel was repeating the same error. Yet the equivalent of this comment was made by ancient Israel's prophets on their own people's sufferings under the empires of Assyria and Babylon.

No Christian can dare to discuss what may, or may not, be the truth about twentieth-century Jewry; Christians have ill-treated Jews too terribly. But there is a people to whom the extraordinary words of Jeremiah (for example) are now piercingly relevant. It is the only other people which has ever claimed to be the heir of the Old Testament's promises. It is the Christian people. The class divisions of ancient Israel, which those prophets saw as weakening the whole social structure, were trivial compared with the contrast between the exploiters and the exploited in modern 'Christian' nations. And ancient Israel's pathetic attempts to play power politics, which those prophets saw as an invitation to catastrophe, amounted to sheer pacifism beside the wars which have been blessed by 'Christian' preachers in modern times. Christendom lies in disarray today; and the most apt commentary on the current decline of the rich white man's religion (or pseudo-religion) has been stored up for centuries by Jeremiah and the other prophets of the Old Testament.

Inevitably the Christians who have seen judgement beginning in the household of God have been accused of rocking the boat. But the most creative of the many changes taking place in the worldwide Church in our time is the growth of a new humility, a new feeling that God has been right to punish the 'Christian' North for its social injustice, militarist nationalism and sentimental piety. That feeling does not get the big congregations back; the City of God, once so full of people, still lies deserted. But at least many Christians have taken the step of acknowledging the truth in the prophecy against them.

A study of the Old Testament is clearly no incentive to an easy optimism. The true prophets were then burdened with unpopular forebodings about the sins of their societies, about the suicidal divisions in the world around them, and about the moral and physical ruin of the people of God; and so it has always been. Those who in the nineteenth century under Tsarism foresaw the Russian Revolution, those who in the twentieth century have had the insight to see the vengeance coming on the Europe of the '30s or the America of the '60s, and Søren Kirkegaard who stands at the head of the prophets of both centuries with his early warning of the doom of Christendom—such are the gloomy men who are (retrospectively) acknowledged to have inherited the mantles of the true prophets.

However, when we are inclined to despair under the prophets' denunciations—and who can be alive today without being tempted to despair?—we are wise to explore the Old Testament further. We then notice an emphasis which is not to be found so prominently in the fashionable 'protest' movement of the political or religious Left. This is the advice to the individual to act justly, to love mercy and to walk wisely.

In one way this emphasis on the quality of personal life increases our depression, and not only because our private failures now come home to us with such cruel insistence. It is human nature—not a particular ordering of society—that is being attacked. The really radical protest of Israel's prophetic movement was against the greed and pride behind the social sins. That exposes much modern 'protest' as facile, for if the heart is sick then no political panacea goes deep enough to cure it. But, in another way, the emphasis on personal integrity can give us some hope. The true prophets have seen in the societies they were denouncing some people who, however obscure, were just, merciful and wise. Always and everywhere there has been the salt of the earth, even in Dietrich Bonhoeffer's Germany or Boris Pasternak's Russia or Alan Paton's South Africa or Norman Mailer's America. Even in the polluted temple there has been the poor widow, praying and giving her all.

Unlike some of our contemporaries, the true prophets have seen this faithful remnant. They have therefore never enjoyed their denunciations, for they have seen what the statisticians could not see; and they have honoured and loved what they have seen. Like Jeremiah, they have wished to God that they had never been called to so uncongenial a task. Like Hosea, they have shown in their private lives that theirs has been a prophecy born of self-sacrifice, self-discipline and compassion. True prophecy is a prophecy of love.

The true prophet entrusts the future to this faithful remnant, however small, and is right to do so. For one thing, it is the true prophet who gets remembered. The people of Israel, for all their sins, included some who were proud that prophets had been among them. To that fact we owe the amazing inclusion of the true prophets in the national literature. In the humiliation of exile, some Jews had the courage to collect the prophets' warnings of disaster; and, in the narrow-minded days of small things back in Palestine after the exile, other Jews preserved Second Isaiah's ecstatic universalism. Hearing such prophecies of doom and restoration read and expounded, and praying in response, was the business of the synagogues emerging during and after the great exile; and it is an encouragement to remember that the synagogue of Nazareth shaped the mind of Jesus. It does not now seem unreasonable to hope that as some modern people, however few, meditate on the warnings and promises of our own true prophets, a better Church—one closer to the faith of the Old Testament at its best, and to Jesus of Nazareth—will be formed by a new remnant. If necessary, this will come after many further disasters to our social and religious institutions.

3

Above all, the emphasis on the personal in the prophets was important because the God whom they glimpsed and announced was intensely personal. They saw him, as Second Isaiah did, holding the oceans in the palm of his hand and all the soil of the earth in a basket, weighing the mountains and thinking no more of nations than of drops from a bucket. But they also thought he cared. They seemed to hear:

> Can a woman forget the infant at her breast,
> or a loving mother the child of her womb?
> Even these forget, yet I will not forget you.

No question is more important for mankind than the question whether the prophets' God was real or an illusion. They believed that the real God upheld the remnant left after the tragedies; and that he was ultimately in control despite the tragedies. That assurance is conspicuously absent from most modern comments on society. It is also lacking in much current religion. Yet one is driven to ask whether a sufficiently powerful protest in the crisis of our time can be based on economics or sociology—or on a different religion. Recent experience seems to suggest that without a touch of 'thus saith the Lord' even the protest against social injustice loses much of its power; and the current condition of Marxist-Leninist orthodoxy does not prove that Karl Marx hit on a completely satisfactory substitute for his ancestors' faith. Certainly one consequence of the feebleness of the conception of God held, or half-held, by discouraged believers is that they do not expect that he will ever again send an army of servants crying aloud with his message.

When we ask what experience made the prophets of ancient Israel so confident of their God, the answer is clear—and clearly relevant to our own needs. It was the experience of life unified religiously. The religion was not merely formal. Some of the most vigorous criticisms of formal religion ever made came from these men, as from Isaiah:

> No more shall you trample my courts.
> The offer of your gifts is useless,
> the reek of sacrifices is abhorrent to me.
> New moons and sabbaths and assemblies,
> sacred seasons and ceremonies, I cannot endure.

Nor is the religion of the prophets to be identified with the informal religion which is merely a celebration of the pleasures of life, the religion of prosperity and strength, the religion which whips up the emotions but in the last analysis worships nature or one's community or oneself. That kind of religion was denounced passionately as being idolatry. It was the religion which already grew out of the soil of Palestine; it was, for example, the religion of sex and crops associated with the worship of Baal. And the prophets of Israel fought it to the death. Theirs was an intensely moral religion, for it trusted man's moral sense as the best clue to the understanding of life—but it was not mere morality. The religion of the prophets was the experience of life as a single reality dominated by the reality of the single, personal, active God. When those who formally worshipped still used dishonest weights and measures, defrauded widows and oppressed the poor, their conduct mattered because daily life ought to be ordered in relation to the real God. To people who thought they were being religious when they were in fact being self-indulgent, the prophets protested that there was one divine reality, demanding a clean life. In the last eleven chapters of the Book of Isaiah, as the great days of prophecy were closing, and when many tragedies and disappointments had overtaken Israel, a voice rose, with a pure simplicity:

> . . . if you feed the hungry from your own plenty
>   and satisfy the needs of the wretched,
> then your light will rise like dawn out of darkness
>   and your dusk be like noonday;
> the Lord will be your guide continually
> and will satisfy your needs in the shimmering heat.

When we ask why the prophets were sure that it was 'the Lord' who guided them, the answer is that the common human experience of finding that the divine reality is personal (or more than personal) was their experience, only it was felt so intensely that it fused and became fire. While priests and kings believed that 'the Lord' could be ignored in practice, they could not believe it. They themselves were furiously indignant at the injustice around them, and particularly at the corruption of religion. They could not believe that the divine reality, single and personal, was indifferent. They were men with great energies; they did not speculate but threw themselves into their times. They could not believe that their God was less alive or less active. And they were men with iron wills. They could not believe that the ultimate reality was weaker. Jeremiah knew his own strength, and affirmed that it had been given by his God for his task:

> This day I make you a fortified city,
>   a pillar of iron, a wall of bronze,
>   to stand fast against the whole land . . .

Their experience was the opposite of sentimental. Often they felt compelled to reject the sentimentalities of religious optimism, as Amos did:

> Fools who long for the day of the Lord,
> what will the day of the Lord mean to you?
> It will be darkness, not light.
> It will be as when a man runs from a lion,
>   and a bear meets him,

or turns into a house and leans his hand on the wall,
and a snake bites him.

They often felt compelled to incur violent unpopularity and utter loneliness (Elijah's 'I alone am left . . .'), because they felt compelled to attack the corrupt society where they themselves lived and to foretell their own nation's defeat. The God they served had become their people's enemy—and was a cruelly hard taskmaster for his servants the prophets. This God was known to be personal because he was known to be angry. But they felt this God in their own personalities, like a pain they could not remove. So Jeremiah confessed:

Whenever I said, 'I will call him to mind no more,
nor speak his name again',
then his word was imprisoned in my body,
like a fire blazing in my heart . . .

Much of the truth in the message of the prophets of ancient Israel was expressed in the Indian idea of *karma*. Actions have consequences. Wrong actions bring evil consequences. But the prophets' proclamation of the wrath of the holy and just God was a more vivid and compelling statement of this truth, because it was a statement in urgently personal terms. It made men listen to the heartbeat of history because it told them that there was in history something like a heart. It was also a statement which made it a little easier to say how men might escape from the endless chain of the consequences of their wrong actions. The idea of *karma* makes right actions the only solution. The prophets of Israel were also practical, from first to last. They demanded righteousness and accepted no substitute.

Spare me the sound of your songs;
I cannot endure the music of your lutes.
Let justice roll on like a river
and righteousness . . .

But bitter experience taught Israel that to expect human beings to live by their own efforts at a high enough level was not being practical. The consciousness of personal sin grew as the national history remained disappointing—as Jerusalem was not saved from enemies, as the returning exiles did not walk into glory. At the same time the hope grew of a new initiative from God. A chain of *karma* cannot take a new initiative, but an angry God can be seen to be the God who acts. He can also be seen to be in deepest fact not merely his people's enemy—and therefore not merely his people's judge.

The prophets of Israel have left evidence of the compassion in their own characters. They were not remote or superior. Amos was typical when he told the professional priest, Amaziah, that his own status was an agricultural labourer's: 'I am a herdsman and a dresser of sycamore figs. But the Lord took me as I followed the flock . . .' These men noticed the details of the life around them because they belonged to that life. They defended the average Israelite because they felt an affectionate loyalty to him. They even came to see something which deserved respect in the life of the nations around Israel—as two short 'books' in the Old Testament show enchantingly. The Book of Ruth is a short story told in a period when the Jews were being exhorted to maintain their racial purity; but it rejects all that without an argument, by giving one fact. Ruth, the foreign girl from Moab, was the ancestress of Israel's national hero, King David. The Book of Jonah is another short story, with another great climax. It records that God—the God of the Earth, the God who had spoken by Israel's prophets—loved Nineveh, the Assyrian capital, with its hundred and twenty thousand babies 'who cannot tell their right hand from their left, and cattle without number'.

These prophets, like their fellow-Jews, thoroughly

relished marriage and parenthood; Jeremiah recorded it as a special example of a prophet's suffering that he felt obliged to remain single. They could not believe that the God they experienced was less compassionate than they were, and they drew on family life for images of the divine mercy. Hosea, when he forgave his unfaithful wife, did so in the conviction that God was like a constantly loving husband:

> But now listen,
> I will woo her, I will go with her into the wilderness and comfort her . . .

And Hosea derived from his experience of being a father his most influential insight into what it must be like to be God:

> When Israel was a boy, I loved him;
> I called my son out of Egypt . . .
> It was I who taught [him] to walk . . .

And one of the earliest of the great prophets, Amos, already saw that the compassion of God for his children did not cover Israel only. Amos taught that the God of Israel had an interest in other nations, and a power to shape their destinies. This applied even to the bitterly hated Philistines and Aramaeans. In every nation's story there was the escape, the exodus.

> Did I not bring Israel up from Egypt,
> The Philistines from Caphtor, the Aramaeans from Kir?

The most important legacy left by the prophets of Israel was the hope in a new development—not to disclose a supernatural 'other' world (the prophets were not interested in that), but to vindicate the character of God as Husband and Father in the midst of the history of this Earth.

VII

JESUS: FACT?

I

The Jesus who really lived in first-century Palestine was a man who assured his contemporaries that the new development they awaited from God was about to occur, and had indeed already begun. This historical reality has been obscured both by the presentation of Jesus as a figure belonging only to the supernatural 'other' world and by the modern presentation of a secular Christ.

The traditional story of Jesus is usually thought by modern people to be full of legends because it is full of miracles. These miracles were (it is thought) regarded as dramatic interventions in the natural order, designed to impress everyone as divine. Most modern people find such miracles incredible. The claims that Jesus was conceived without a human father, that his corpse walked out of his tomb and eventually disappeared into a cloud in the sky, and that he inspired his first follower to speak foreign languages by sending a wind and flames of fire—these are claims which seem to be among the most important parts of the traditional story, not least because they are presented in the parts of the Bible associated with the festivals of Christmas, Easter and Whitsun. Other miracle stories crowd the brief accounts of the years between this miraculous entry and departure. Jesus is reported as creating bread, changing water into wine, walking on water, killing a fig tree with a curse, and healing many diseases, even including death, with a word. The figure about whom such stories are repeated often seems to be a figure so shrouded in legends that he is unrecognizable as a real man.

Even more baffling to modern minds is the traditional emphasis on the status of Jesus in the supernatural world. Christian orthodoxy seems to have claimed that Jesus was not really a man but was the eternal Second Person of the Trinity, 'through' or 'by' whom 'all things were made' in the creation of the universe. This Second Person's relationship with the First and Third Persons, both before and after the creation, has been discussed at great length. Eventually the Second Person 'took' human nature in the 'Incarnation' (the Enfleshment) and retained it after the 'Ascension' into 'heaven'—with consequences for eternity which have also aroused great discussion. But the greatest passions in the history of Christian doctrine have been aroused by the discussion about the way in which the two natures, human and divine, were joined during the Incarnation. During this debate large numbers of Christians excommunicated each other as heretics. Those who believed in the formula which was eventually agreed to be orthodox had no doubt that others would 'perish everlastingly'.

Why was the Incarnation necessary? The traditional answer seems to go like this. The First Person of the Trinity was angry with man's sin, and was either unwilling or unable to forgive man until an appropriate penalty had been paid. The Second Person of the Trinity was born in order to die, thus offering to the divine justice the sacrifices of a perfect human life and a death infinitely full of physical and spiritual suffering. This sacrifice was satisfactory to God 'the Father', and those who believe that it was are entitled to claim that it is the substitute for the penalty due on their own sins. Those who do not so believe appear to have been left to join those perishing everlastingly; perhaps (as some very eminent theologians have speculated) because they were anyway doomed by a divine decree. An exception has been made in favour of any of those who had died before the sacrifice of the death of the Second Person, but who accepted its merits on hearing about it between the first Good Friday and the first Easter Day in the supernatural 'other' world.

It is understandable that there has been a reaction in modern times against this traditional account of Jesus. Instead, the historical Jesus has been interpreted by what has been called 'Christian atheism'. Those who adopt this position are convinced that it is hopeless to try to restore belief in the supernatural 'other' world or in any divine reality, but that Jesus should still be regarded as the supreme teacher of ethics, who taught chiefly by living for others. In recent years a number of ex-theologians have written books working out this attitude in the 'Death of God theology', but throughout this century many laymen who have wished to be called Christians have quietly based their lives on this solution of the problem, holding that morality is what matters. The trouble with this solution, however, is that any Christian morality depends on a reverent attitude to Jesus, and on a high valuation of his teaching. But when we study that teaching, we find a man who based everything on God, like the prophets of ancient Israel who were clearly regarded by him as his predecessors. It would be far more accurate to say that he lived for God than that he lived for other people, because on the evidence we have he was no more a social worker than he was a millionaire. If this total dependence on God was fundamentally mistaken, the conclusion seems inevitable that a fresh, secular basis has to be found for modern morality—and new teachers have to be found to expound and embody it.

Many of the values symbolized in the figure of Jesus can, admittedly, be discovered without straying beyond the limits of the secular. They appeal to secular humanists; in them there is a kind of natural religion, within the limits of reason alone. We see in Jesus a happy man, a lover of nature and the simple life of the home, a poet of glory in the commonplace. A poor man, a village carpenter, an Asian Jew, the brother of the wretched of the earth; a compassionate man, with the imagination to know the distress and dignity of those worse off than himself. A noble man, who put man's spiritual needs above bread. A man of integrity and a brave man, with the courage to obey his own conscience in this spiritual struggle against inherited codes and against the religious and political authorities. A free man, who made others free. A man who risked and sacrificed everything in order to live and die a life and death of love. A man who could tell those who would listen to love one another as he had loved them. A man whose personality gradually attracted into the fellowship of his followers men and women, rich and poor, fishermen and intellectuals, Jews and Gentiles. A man who has been powerful, often supremely powerful, through nineteen centuries. A man who is greatly respected by atheists, Muslims, Hindus and Communists, and adored as the ideal man by people in every country of the modern world. A man who still fascinates. The story of that life has inspired what are acknowledged as the best human qualities in our civilization, and it will be a notable day if ever that story is replaced. While it has this asset—Jesus the man, as the symbol of man being human—Christianity will not die completely, however little may be left of its institutions and doctrines.

The institutions of Christianity have declined, and are likely to decline further, because they do not remind people of that story with enough simplicity, courage, compassion and practical love. The doctrines of Christianity have often been rejected or quietly forgotten because they seem implausible additions to the reality in that story.

Individuals who call themselves Christians are condemned because the name is not for them existential: they have not identified their lives with Christ's. And yet there is more to be said than that. The institutions of Christianity, for all their failures, have been places where a good many people have gradually conformed their lives to that life, and the history of the twentieth century would have been more squalid without such holiness. And we may dare to say something else about the institutions of Christianity. They have preserved certain doctrines. However unsatisfactorily, these doctrines have related the life of saints to a mysterious source—a source more mysterious than any ethical ideal within the secular understanding. It may turn out to have been an advantage that the institutions and doctrines of Christianity were so out of keeping with the twentieth century; eventually they may produce something very precious by being irritants, like the grit in the oyster. The chief duty of those who guard the traditions of Christianity may be to keep going, although not inflexibly, in the hope that a happier age will use what has been preserved together with many new treasures.

By this is meant not only Christianity's role in keeping alive human values amid technology; we also refer to something even more difficult. We refer to the answers to those very old questions about the ultimate meaning of beauty and love, of existence and death. For let us be frank about Jesus. Some of the values which secular people have in mind when they say that life can have a meaning were *not* embodied in him. He was not a great political leader or economic reformer. He was not an effective revolutionary; on the evidence we have, he did not even intend to be one. He was not a scientist or artist. He was not even, so far as we know, a great carpenter. There is no evidence that he was handsome or athletic.

He had no wife or children to love. He died young, and he died very painfully. A man of sorrows; a man of mystery. Perhaps he made the wrong choice when he gave up his useful carpentry? But in the sorrow and the mystery, his followers have claimed to have found a reality more fascinating than all the glamour of the world: the reality of the God on whom Jesus depended.

2

Evidently we must recover the real Jesus; and the first thing we must say about the traditional pictures of Jesus is that they were intended to express the real uniqueness of the historical Jesus and the real mystery surrounding him. In fact, Jesus has defied description because he does not belong to any class of men. What he claimed, what he was, what he did—these facts set him apart, alone. No other religious leader has closely resembled him, except perhaps for some of the Christian saints, who completely depended on him and worshipped him. His uniqueness is a matter of history, and does not need to be supported by speculation about what he was doing before he was born.

The story of the 'Virgin Birth' of Jesus was presumably first told in order to express the belief that the life of Jesus was utterly unique and was the most important part of the new initiative now coming from God. The deepest reality in the life of Jesus seemed to be the fresh activity of God the Husband and Father. The records which survive show that Jesus himself thought this and that his followers soon came to share his conviction. Both Paul and John, the two greatest theologians in the first Christian generation, expressed this conviction without mentioning the story of the 'Virgin Birth', but when we know that many stories were told in the ancient world about divine saviours born without human fathers we can understand why Luke and Matthew told such stories about Jesus—although Matthew began by showing the descent of Jesus from Abraham through Joseph, to our confusion. The great beauty of these stories of Bethlehem does not mean that they are accurate history.

The stories about Jesus after his death are harder to assess. On the one hand, many stories circulated in the ancient world about dying and rising gods, and although those were pagan stories, devout Jews shared the belief that men would rise from their graves when God took the expected new initiative. As the Book of Daniel put it,

> many of those who sleep in the dust of the earth
> will wake, some to everlasting life.
> and some to the reproach of eternal abhorrence.

It is possible to regard all the stories about the appearances of Jesus after his death as legends based on the Jewish belief that resurrections were inevitable, and we could understand the appeal of such legends in the non-Jewish world also.

On the other hand, we know for certain that the first Christian generation was extremely confident and active, although the accounts which it gave of its own leaders' behaviour when they had been the companions of Jesus never pretended that there had been any sense of firm faith or clear purpose. Something must have happened to change the first followers of Jesus, and that something cannot have been the death of Jesus by itself. Jesus was executed by methods well calculated by the Romans to degrade criminals and to horrify the criminals' associates. There must have been some experience *after* the death of Jesus. What was experienced may have been a part of the phenomena which are investigated nowadays by 'psychical research', but if so the experience of the followers of Jesus transformed them in a way which has never been observed among students of psychic phenomena or among those who claim that they communicate with the dead through spiritualism. What happened to them must have hit them as a real experience. We can well understand why Christians came to insist that it had been more like a body than a ghost. Indeed, we have reason to respect the faith of those present-day Christians who maintain that the resurrection of Jesus was physical —that his tomb really was found to be empty because his corpse had risen. That faith amounts to a belief that the development of the world spurted forward on the first Easter Day, with the result that a corpse was first revived and then dematerialized without a nuclear explosion. Although it is a very strange faith, it is based on the conviction that in the spiritual development of mankind the life of Jesus, including his victory over death, achieved a breakthrough so stupendous that its consequence—the physical resurrection of Jesus—was in some sense natural. The risen body showed that a new era in 'creation' had arrived. However, if the reality of the Easter experience is admitted, and if the experience is regarded as the most important moment in all evolution, we may still remain agnostics about the precise nature of what was experienced. That seems a sensible attitude to the reports made by 'psychical research' about phenomena allegedly experienced in our own time—how much more sensible is it as a reaction to reports made in the first century A.D. after events which the reporters themselves said were unique!

The earliest account of the resurrection of Jesus which we possess was written down by Paul for the Christians in Corinth. It would not enable us to be sure about exactly what was experienced, even if it had been written nearer the event. It says that Jesus was 'buried' and 'raised to life on the third day', and that 'he appeared to over five hundred of our brothers at once, most of whom are still alive'. This suggests a claim that the resurrection was physical. But the climax in the list of the appearances of the risen Jesus is that 'in the end he appeared even to me'—and it is nowhere claimed that Paul saw any risen body. On the basis of belief that Christ was 'raised to life', Paul proceeds to affirm that 'all will be brought to life', but he emphasizes that 'flesh and blood can never possess the kingdom of God', and what he expects is a 'spiritual body'.

The ends of the four gospels also show that their authors were well aware of the mystery surrounding this unique experience after the death of Jesus. Luke, for example, tells of a body which was unrecognized as that of Jesus, but which vanished and, when it appeared again, was thought to be a ghost before it ate a piece of fish. It is clear that stories told in different Christian communities appear in the four gospels. These stories, which jump from Jerusalem to Galilee, cannot be fitted together with each other (or with Paul's list) to make a coherent narrative showing precisely where, when and how the appearances took place. But any uncertainty left about details evidently did not worry the writers. As John wrote, the events were recorded as 'signs'—'in order that you may hold the faith'.

It seems probable that, if summoned back for a modern conversation, these writers would have agreed that some of the details in their stories were not scientifically accurate but were symbolic. Luke certainly described the coming of the Holy Spirit as being 'in tongues *like* flames of fire' after 'a noise *like* that of a strong driving wind' (the italics are ours). And it seems equally probable that the stories of the miracles performed by Jesus before his death are equally full of symbols because they, too, were told in order to be 'signs' on the road to faith in an age which accepted supernatural interference in nature's course. What actually happened is in many cases lost. It may have been something ordinary: Jesus presiding over a meal for many followers, Jesus at a wedding party, Jesus walking by the lake, Jesus using a fig-tree to illustrate his teaching, Jesus transforming a sick person's attitude from despair to faith and therefore speeding or even accomplishing the physical recovery (for the mind has strange powers over the body). It seems reasonable to suppose that in the telling of these stories numbers have grown, the deadliness of the disease has been exaggerated, and other dramatic effects have been heightened. For example, it seems reasonable to think that the story of the miraculous coin in the mouth of the fish began as advice to pay tax peacefully after earning the money as a fisherman. But in no case do the details matter vitally to us. It would not be supremely important to us even if we were to be sure that Jesus had stilled a storm on a lake.

It also seems probable that, if pressed by modern analysis of religious language, the most orthodox of Christian theologians would have admitted that all their doctrines about Jesus were attempts to use symbols in order to speak about a mystery, the only alternative being a complete silence. Certainly we can understand how the symbolic language of the doctrine of the Holy Trinity grew out of the solid experience of the Christians. This was experience of the divine reality as single and personal, righteous and loving, and it was experience coming to them in three ways: through their general experience of nature and history, through their particular experience of the life, death and victory of Jesus, and through their own immediate experience of a new, spiritual unity and power in the Christian Church. This experience was reflected clearly in many places where Paul, for example, was not writing formal theology, as when he said goodbye to the Christians in Corinth: 'The grace of the Lord Jesus Christ, and the love of God, and the fellowship of the

Holy Spirit, be with you all'.

Having found the life of Jesus the supreme example of the activity of God, these Christians found his character the supreme illumination of the character of God; and since he was human, alive in the ordinary physical world, they used this as the best clue they had to the mystery of human life in the universe. They were sure that God had expressed himself through Jesus. They began to see the same pattern running through the rest of history and even through the great enigma, nature. Paul, knowing 'the liberty and splendour of the children of God', compared the whole history of the universe with a birth. The comparison has meant much to twentieth-century Christians who have found that their vision of the splendour of man's evolution has brought some meaning to the evolving nature out of which, so strangely, man has come. Paul wrote, 'the whole created universe groans in all its parts as in the pangs of childbirth'. John used the current term 'Word' (in Greek *Logos*), meaning the expression of God giving everything its basic pattern. It may help us more to think of a programme in a computer. The divine Word has finally been expressed in 'flesh', in a human life—'and we saw his glory', glory which now shows that the same divine Word, the same programme, is in everything. Jesus shows that *a man* is coming out of the womb of nature, out of the mess of history—and so he reveals the secret code which explains all existence.

The shining of this Word as light in the darkness has not been effortless. John hinted at past battles when he wrote that 'the darkness has never mastered it', and he wrote his gospel in order to present the conflict between Jesus and the darkness—a conflict that demanded all that Jesus had to give. It was inevitable that Christians such as Paul and John, seeing Jesus like this, should connect this self-sacrifice with the familiar system of sacrifices in the Jewish and pagan temples—sacrifices which were deliberately expensive for an agricultural community. But we who are not familiar with the spectacle of a farmer sacrificing his lamb are helped more by comparing Jesus in his battle with a sight all too familiar to us: a soldier sacrificing his life. Paul and John found it natural to think of God accepting the self-sacrifice of Jesus, much as the sacrifice offered in a temple would be accepted by the divinity worshipped there. But Paul's deepest insight was that God was in the life of Jesus, rather than on a great white throne above it. 'From first to last this has been the work of God . . . God was in Christ reconciling the world to himself.' The deepest insight of John was that the glory of the enfleshed Word of God shone on the cross. 'God is love; and his love was disclosed to us in this . . .' The deepest truth about the self-sacrifice of Jesus is that it embodied the self-sacrifice of God, placarding God's love by a man's broken body. The deepest truth about the human response to the cross is that it is the response of those who now love God because they love back.

It was also inevitable that the world-transforming results of the life of Jesus should be compared with two other great moments of happiness. The first was the repayment of debts to a moneylender. The debtor was not a free agent; he was in the moneylender's power, and often was further humiliated because he thought it only just that he should be. The payment of debts brought dignity as well as solvency. The other great moment was the payment which bought the freeing of a slave. This 'redemption' released a human life from degradation. We in the modern world are still familiar with debts and with degrading conditions of employment, but we seldom experience releases so dramatic, and the presentation of the work of Jesus by a comparison with those moments has lost much of its impact on us. What many people in our time have experienced is liberation from an occupying power—the conqueror or the colonist. This is something which the subjects of the Roman Empire did not experience in the first century, but nineteen centuries later Jesus the Liberator means more than Jesus the Redeemer.

All the evidence suggests that Jesus was acutely aware of the spiritual dangers faced by those around him. Such dangers were increased by his coming, for by rejecting him men showed that they preferred darkness to light. Jesus saw the crisis which his coming created—and he saw the road ahead of him and his few followers as hard and narrow. To describe the self-inflicted exclusion from the joy of God, he used the usual pictures drawn from the repulsive sight of Jerusalem's rubbish-dump: the perpetually smouldering fire, the maggots. But the response which he wanted was a whole man's turning to the light. It was not the acceptance of a theological formula. He believed that it was possible for people to accept the forgiveness of God without holding any theory about his own life or death; he often said so. And his hope was that his life, and his death close to that rubbish-dump, would be for the benefit of 'many'. He foresaw 'many' sitting down for the final banquet of life with God—the banquet made possible by the pouring out of his life blood. John's gospel, which is full of stern warnings about the consequences of rejecting Jesus, rightly records that the purpose of Jesus was 'that men may have life, and may have it in all its fullness'.

The Christian use of the cross as a symbol of the divisions between men is therefore a horrible travesty of the original and permanent meaning of the death of Jesus. In a scene which sums up the tortures inflicted on each other by men blinded by prejudice, hatred and fear, Jesus embodied the inexhaustible love which is the supreme characteristic of the single divine reality. By the total expenditure of himself, he did it in a way which draws many to accept the Father and all people in love. John was, we may hope, right to foresee that ultimately, as they come to see Jesus, this will draw 'all men'.

3

Jesus was a man who prayed to God. There is an authentic echo of his humility in his protest recorded by Mark: 'Why do you call me good? No one is good except God alone'. But other authentic echoes of his voice make clear his claim to a unique authority. So far from subjecting himself completely to the discipline of the religious code of his time (and many people have become holy in that way, while Jesus himself was regularly devout), he claimed the right and the power to set aside the Law of Moses which he, like his fellow-Jews, believed had been dictated by God. He deliberately defied the prohibition of work on the Sabbath, the holy day which more than any other custom had made the Jews what they were. So far from stressing his own sinfulness (as all the saints have always done), Jesus claimed the right and the power to liberate people from their sense of sinfulness. He violently criticized the religious leadership of his day, and ate and drank with notorious sinners. While in these ways turning the religion of his day upside down, he warned his hearers that eternal life depended on the response to his message. For all his humility, he was a man sure of his special relationship with God. He spoke of his work of healing as driving out devils by the finger of God. Even in his dying despair, his cry was to '*my* God, *my* God'.

His followers naturally wished to understand more of this special relationship with God. John's gospel for the most part puts into the mouth of Jesus the results of Christian experience, although it contains an element of solid history; and in it the demand that Jesus should be acknowledged for what he is in himself looms much larger than in the other three gospels. But Mark, Luke and Matthew show Jesus talking about himself only incidentally.

They report that he accepted the two Jewish titles 'Son of Man' and *Messiah* (in Greek, *Chrestos*). Many scholars who have examined the gospels with minute care do not, however, believe that in fact Jesus ever used such titles about himself. The evidence is too complicated to discuss here, and anyway it is clear that if Jesus did call himself 'Son of Man' or *Messiah* he did so in a sense very different from the generally accepted sense. To Jews, the 'Son of Man' was *the* man who at the end of history would represent the righteous Jews in the final ascent to God. The Book of Daniel, in one of its 'visions of the night', had left the picture of 'one like a man coming with the clouds of heaven; he approached the Ancient in Years and was presented to him. Sovereignty and glory and kingly power were given to him, so that all people and nations of every language should serve him . . .' *Messiah*, meaning the Anointed or the King, was a figure belonging more clearly to the soil of Palestine, where, it was believed, he would lead the Jews victoriously in history's final battles. If such titles were at all fitting for Jesus, it was only after a radical modification. 'Foxes have their holes, the birds their roosts; but the Son of Man has nowhere to lay his head'. The only occasions on which Jesus was acknowledged as King of the Jews were in the small procession into Jerusalem ('*Hosanna*! Blessings on the coming kingdom of our father David!') and as part of the mockery in the execution which inevitably followed that demonstration. Far more appropriate to Jesus was the picture left by Second Isaiah of an executed prisoner as the representative of Jewish suffering:

He had no beauty, no majesty to draw our eyes . . .
He was despised, he shrank from the sight of men, tormented and humbled by suffering . . .

Almost certainly this picture of God's suffering servant helped Jesus, as no other inherited picture did, to see his task. But it is clear that no single picture in the Old Testament dominated his mind. His task was new, as was his message.

The novelty was summed up in the form of prayer in which he addressed the divine reality. He called God 'Daddy'—for that is the proper translation of the Aramaic *Abba* which Jesus used and which Paul quoted twice in his surviving letters. *Abba* was the intimate word used by Jewish children to their fathers. It was fondly believed to be what a baby said, although grown-up sons and daughters could still use the term. The comparison of God with a human father had been made, but no one before Jesus had dared to address God in this way—at least, no one we know about. The Jewish sense of reverence was too deep. Jesus had already formed an intense reverence for God before he began teaching, as we can see from his resistance to the common temptations which appeal to a religion which is not God-centred. This, surely, is the meaning of the story that immediately after his baptism, when alone in the wilderness, he rejected as devilish any idea that he should concentrate on feeding the hungry, on getting the backing of the powerful, or on impressing the silly by miracles. As he entered his public life, Jesus had already made completely his own the teaching of the Old Testament that the knowledge of God's reality is necessary food for man's real life; that God alone is to be taken with a final seriousness; and that the God who is real and ultimate is not to be put to the test in man's emergencies or expected to show how useful he is to man's selfish schemes. Jesus cared passionately that God alone should be regarded as sacred, his name alone 'holy' or 'hallowed'. But Jesus expressed this reverence by calling God by the name which he had used for Joseph.

The records of the life of Jesus show that this astonishing custom developed in the hours, including whole nights, which he spent in prayer. Occasionally we can glimpse the content of the prayer, and each time we can see how this particular kind of prayer strengthened the intimacy of this new understanding of God's Fatherhood. Jesus prayed for his followers and specially for Simon Peter, treating them as close brothers. When some of his followers 'came back jubilant', Jesus 'exulted' and cried, 'I thank thee, *Abba*, Lord of heaven and earth . . .' But the prayer could be for those who were not followers, but who still deserved the Father's pity. '*Abba*, forgive them . . .' And the prayer could be for himself, first asking for a favour and then trustfully accepting the Father's will. '*Abba*, if it be thy will, take this cup away from me. Yet not my will but thine be done.' '*Abba*, into thy hands I commit my spirit.'

Because God was experienced by Jesus as *Abba*, Jesus became convinced that God would be close to him even in degradation and death—and that God would act to make his Fatherhood more plain to him and to all others. For Jesus could not believe that the divine reality was less fatherly than men. 'Is there a father among you who will offer his son a snake when he asks for fish, or a scorpion when he asks for an egg?' And Jesus was clear about what would be the appropriate gift, the equivalent of fish or an egg, to a tragic mankind. *Abba* would act so that he was obeyed as King of Earth, and his reality would be shown by his rule.

For the past fifty years or more, almost all scholars who have studied the gospels scientifically have agreed that this theme is at their centre, however much they may have disagreed about minor points or about the interpretation of this original theme in relation to later developments. The theme is, indeed, the first sound heard from Jesus in the first of the four gospels to be written (Mark): 'The time has come; the kingdom of God is upon you; repent, and believe the Gospel.' The answer to the historical question about Jesus stares us in the face. All other teaching, spiritual or social, is secondary. The message of Jesus is the news of the kingdom of God resulting from the Fatherhood of God.

The miracle stories are understood by almost all scholars in connection with this message. These scholars think both that Jesus possessed unusual powers of 'spiritual' (more accurately psychosomatic, spirit-and-body) healing, and that he exercised these powers in order to show by deed that the kingdom of God was indeed 'upon' that generation. His answer to John the Baptist's inquiry confirms this. John, disturbed by the quietness of Jesus's work, had sent messengers from prison to ask whether he was indeed 'the one who is to come'—*Messiah*, inaugurating the final kingdom of God. The reply of Jesus, as we have it, lists many of the blessings which had been promised by the great prophets and by many coming after them who had looked forward to the kingdom of God. 'Go and tell John what you hear and see: the blind recover their sight, the lame walk, the lepers are made clean, the deaf hear, the dead are raised to life, the poor are hearing the good news . . .'

The idea of the kingdom of God was familiar to those who heard Jesus. It was not the idea of a kingdom with frontiers, although Israel lay at the centre; it was the belief that God would rule. Some of the contemporaries and near-contemporaries of Jesus indulged in luxuriant speculations about the details of the good things to come.

Jesus was not among these. They particularly indulged in the thought that Jews would have a monopoly of the good things. Jesus contradicted that expectation. They claimed to know the day and the hour when the rule of God would fully arrive. Jesus did not. If this seemed necessary they were prepared to force God's hand, compelling him to 'bring in the kingdom' by creating an emergency so great that God would feel obliged to act if he was not to fail the test. That was not the spirit in which Jesus lived or died. Naturally Jesus used many of the images familiar to his contemporaries when he announced the coming kingdom of God, and naturally he hoped and believed that this kingdom would come completely within the lifetime of his own generation; some strong expressions of that hope and belief have been preserved. But because the teaching of Jesus about the kingdom of God was not limited as contemporary expectations were limited, the essence of that teaching has survived the facts that Jesus died, and that his generation died, without seeing the full kingdom on Earth.

Superficially the teaching of Jesus is now dated, for the images in which it was expressed have not remained images drawn from daily life and from common, contemporary hopes. They began to be dated even within the period covered by the New Testament. In Paul's letters the phrase 'Son of Man' does not occur at all, and the idea of the kingdom of God is not as prominent as in the gospels. But the message behind the images has not been so obviously dated. At least, many generations have found a reward in considering it, as we shall now do. People have believed Jesus to be 'risen' because they have known him to be relevant. From generation to generation, he has been contemporary.

VIII

JESUS: RELEVANT?

I

For the most part, Jesus taught by short stories. These were stories based on the daily life around him in order to make a point about the coming kingdom of God. Nowhere in Jewish or Christian literature is there a series like them. They were such good stories that many of them were remembered and repeated before they were written down in the gospels which we have. They always have been remembered. But their background faded into being history, and often their original points ceased to be obvious or obviously relevant. When they were retold, they were re-interpreted. That happened on a large scale in the ages when Christianity emphasized the supernatural 'other' world as Jesus had not done. The process had already begun to occur by the time the gospels were written.

At that time, Christians were preoccupied by their duty to hold their faith despite the delay in the full coming of the kingdom of God. The gospels were directed at this spiritual situation where the disappointed had to be warned to persevere. Matthew, for example, worked into his gospel these three sayings: 'Thus will the last be first and first last', 'For though many are invited few are chosen' and 'Keep awake then; for you never know the day or the hour'. He added these sayings to the end of three of the short stories of Jesus. But we can know that these were his additions, for in no case does the saying fit the story.[1]

[1] In the first parable, about the labourers in the vineyard, the order of the queue is not reversed; all end up equal. In the second

Modern scholars have stripped away all these later additions in order to get at the original 'parable', as varnish is stripped from a great painting to reveal the fresh glow of its original colours. But we should not completely condemn all these editors who added their interpretations to the stories, for always the aim was to make the teaching of Jesus, as this was understood, relevant to the needs of a fresh generation. It is right to attempt the same task for our time, but to take care to keep the interpretation as close as possible to the original message. As we pursue this task, we find that the rapid development of the modern world has created a spiritual situation in our age close to the condition of those who heard the parables for the very first time. The position in which we find ourselves is striking: when we have stripped away the first-century hopes that the kingdom of God would come completely in the lifetime of that generation, we find that the message of the parables is still clearly relevant. There is, after all, no need to base Christianity on a fresh foundation to be supplied by the philosophy of some other teacher.

The main difficulty for us is that the original meaning sharply challenges our habits of thought. But it was the same at the beginning. This is shown by the story of the farmer sowing before he ploughed—then the normal practice. Some of the seed fell on the well-trodden footpath, the well-established route taken by all conservatives. That seed was wasted. Some fell on rocky ground where the soil was too shallow to provide proper roots. That part of the crop sprouted quickly—until the sun scorched it. Here, surely, was symbolized the laziness of the progres-

---

parable, about the guests at the wedding, all are invited and admitted In the third parable, about bridesmaids, both the wise and the foolish go to sleep.

sives, eager for quick growth but unable to go deep. Over and over again the trendiness of the progressives has proved too shallow to stand the test. And some of the seed fell on ill-weeded ground. The weeds were not noticeable until they had become thistles sucking in the goodness of the earth. This neatly depicts the compromising attitude in religion as elsewhere, the hope that all one's old habits can be comfortably preserved despite one's new interests. But the point of this parable was that *some* seed reached fertile ground. The message of Jesus was really heard by some.

The original message was of the coming of the kingdom of God. This was news, demanding a new response. It was like new wine, demanding a new wine-skin, or a new piece of cloth, which no thrifty housewife would use to mend old garments because it would shrink too much. And the parables were pleas that people should open their eyes and look. 'In the evening you say, "It will be fine weather, for the sky is red" . . . You know how to interpret the appearance of the sky; can you not interpret the signs of the times?' The hearers of Jesus were being given a last warning. They were, he said, like a man who had been summonsed and was actually on his way to court—with a chance, as he walked with his accuser, to settle the matter before getting involved with the law.

The fig tree casts its leaves in winter; we are told that it was the only tree common in first-century Palestine to do so. 'Look at the fig tree . . . As soon as it buds, you can see for yourselves that summer is near. In the same way when you see all this happening, you may be sure that the kingdom of God is near.' But most of those around Jesus did not see, and were not sure. They were therefore compared with a barren fig tree, about which a man complains that 'for the last three years I have been looking for fruit on this fig tree without finding any'. Their unbelief was tragic, and it suggested that they were like a rotten tree which could never produce good fruit—or like a thistle from which 'you do not gather figs'.

Such was the urgency of the original message. But what does the idea of the kingdom of God mean to us today?

2

Jesus built his analysis of the human situation around the figure of the steward. In modern towns, branch managers are expected to use their own initiative. 'Head office' may be suspicious and in a crisis the top managers may have to intervene, but it is healthy for the local man to feel responsible for his own show. In much the same way, the Palestine which Jesus knew allowed a wide scope to this managerial class of stewards. These men were often deputies for landlords who were absent abroad, and Jesus was easily understood when he began a story: 'A man going abroad . . . called his servants and put his capital in their hands'. According to Jesus, this was the explanation of the apparent absence of God from the affairs of men. God had given them their opportunity, valuing their freedom more highly than they did themselves.

In our own society, some managers are dishonest in fiddling expenses or dodging taxes. In the time of Jesus some of the practices of the managerial class seemed harmless or at least amusing, as in the story of the cunning rascal who was dismissed from his job but who secured the good will of his master's debtors by slashing their bills; he could be commended as a man who paid serious attention to a crisis. But Jesus told a grimmer story of the tenants who embezzled all a vineyard's profits and did not stick at murder; and of the steward who became a drunken tyrant in his master's absence and was therefore 'cut in pieces'. And recognizing that some of the honest are honest because they lack courage, he told the sad story of the little man who was too nervous even to go to the bank, but hid the gold entrusted to him by his master in a hole in the ground. By pointing to such tragedies, Jesus pointed to the abuses of human freedom —and their consequences. It is blindness to read this as a message for the first century only.

One of the most glaring dangers confronting the twentieth century results from coloured people being alienated when in fact their contribution is desperately needed. Asia is not aided effectively enough; as one result, Asia outside Japan is a poor trading partner. American Negroes are underprivileged; American cities are violent. The supreme example is, of course, South Africa—where the labour of the black man is needed in the white man's industry and the white man's home, and where, incidentally, Bantu hearts are needed for transplants into the bodies of advocates of 'separate development', but where, amid surroundings of boundless beauty and opportunity, the black man's hatred is being earned—until vengeance comes. The parable of the good Samaritan was addressed to a Jew as arrogant as any modern advocate of white supremacy. The Jew who first heard that story would identify himself with the man beaten up and robbed by bandits, because this man was another Jew. He would expect the kind of anticlerical story a carpenter from Galilee might tell: the priest was useless, the priest's assistant was equally useless, but a layman gave help. The Jewish hearer would be stabbed in his conscience by the point in the story which Jesus told: the layman who did help was one of the Samaritans who were so thoroughly despised by pure-blooded Jews. The moral of that story is now plain. It was not in the Jew's own interest to love only his fellow-Jew. 'You shall love your neighbour as a man like yourself' is a quotation from Leviticus in the Old Testament, where it refers to 'your brother', 'your fellow-countryman' and 'your kinsfolk'; but the Jew needed the Samaritan—just as the rich white man needs the poor coloured man in the modern world. For Jesus, the first step out of the tragedy of misused freedom was that men should acknowledge their need of one another.

The second step was to acknowledge their need of God. It was the *second* step: those who remembered having cheated another man were advised to get immediately out of the temple, leaving the animal being sacrificed in front of the altar, and those who had not forgiven others were warned not to expect God's forgiveness. But the step towards God was to be taken with an absolute determination.

If people felt that prayer was 'no use'—as so many people do in our time—they must hammer away at it. Jesus was willing to compare the divine Father with a peasant in bed with his children (and animals) asleep around him, or with a judge who would become active only in order to put an end to constant badgering. Jesus did not believe in a God who revealed himself easily or who intervened dramatically. Even in response to the cries of human need, the God whom Jesus revealed was almost endlessly cautious. He was like a farmer who would refuse to weed a field where a crop was already growing, for fear of doing greater damage than any weeds. The slow process, with the seed growing secretly, must be allowed to take its course.

The method chosen by God tested all that was in a man. It was futile to seek God if one was not prepared to pay the price; just as it was futile for a king to embark on a campaign, or even on a building project, without a proper budget. And God's method went on testing. It was futile to think that God would transform even one's own *spiritual* condition at a stroke. One should not be like the man who enthusiastically spring-cleaned his cottage, complacently left it empty, and returned to find that dirty devils had occupied it. The return to God would be step after step, and it would mean a death, perhaps literally.

But in that slow process, God was coming—just as the smallest seed known in Palestine would grow into a shrub yielding both mustard for men and roosts for birds; just as a tiny piece of salted leaven would ferment a whole mass of dough and make it bread.

Accordingly, Jesus said that God was like a burglar breaking into a mud-walled house, or like a bandit forcing his way into a castle. God was like a good shepherd who would not rest until he had brought back a wandering sheep; or like a good employer who was determined that the unemployed should all get a *denarius*, the workman's daily wage, however little they had worked, because a man could not support a family on less. He was like a father determined to welcome a son back from abroad —and so running to meet that son, as very few dignified first-century fathers would do. He was also like a father determined to give a foolish son the best of everything back again. And he was like a father determined not to let any elder brother's resentment stop the celebration. This was the message which Jesus himself acted out when he refused to give up meals with prostitutes and with the racketeers in the Roman Empire's tax system. It is also a message for a later generation which prides itself on being both determined and compassionate, but which is reluctant to believe that the ultimate reality is more so.

No cheerful young citizen of a modern city talks about parties with the zest with which Jesus talked, using the banquet as the great image of God's plan for man.

Jesus used other images. He compared finding the real God with the clink of one's spade against a gleaming treasury of gold buried in a field which one can then buy at a bargain price because no one else knows that the gold is there. He also compared it with the clink of a broom of twigs against a coin lost on the floor of a cottage without windows—a coin which was an essentiai part of the pattern on the head-dress which was a married woman's only dowry. He compared it with a complete release from fantastically vast debts, and with a pearl worth a fortune. But the party, and particularly the wedding feast, was at the centre of Jesus's appeal to the imagination. A party was alive and a pearl was not. Freshly washed garments were needed, and they would show up anyone who came casually in his normal grubby clothes. Lights were needed, and oil for the lamps must be arranged. And guests were needed. If the respectable people to whom the first invitations were addressed did not have the imagination to accept, other guests must be found. This party given by God was not to be halted.

3

To share this vision of life is to see life as the beginning of a banquet. There are many reasons for seeing life in another way; indeed, Christians have been no less emphatic than atheists that life is grim, a tough battle, not a banquet; and also that life is lonely, a solitary pilgrimage, not a party. Christians have, like their Master, resembled children unable to persuade others to join in the game of 'weddings'—or in the game of 'funerals'. For this wedding cannot be entirely carefree, any more than this funeral can be entirely depressing. Face to face with the reality of evil, what reason is there to share Jesus's vision of a glory beyond the tragedy, a wedding after the funeral? If Jesus hoped that the full kingdom of God would come in the lifetime of his generation—and the evidence is that he did—he was wrong. But was he wrong completely in his vision of life as it could be and was already beginning to be? If we think that he was basically right, we may reasonably conclude that it was essential that he should be enthusiastic in order to communicate that vision—and that it was natural that his enthusiasm should lead him to emphasize the urgency of the crisis rather than the possibility that the seed might have to go on growing, more or less secretly, for thousands of millions of years to come.

Only one reason can justify the claim that he was basically right. This is the reason: we have shared to a significant—although not complete—extent the experience of the first Christians which lies behind the New Testament's claim that Jesus is the 'risen' Lord. The most important components of the experience are these: being attracted to Jesus, being willing to take his vision of life seriously, being prepared for the possibility that it may be basically true, being ready to examine the signs, that is, seeing those signs, accepting those signs as the best available clues to the meaning of life for us. Some of the signs of the victory of Jesus lie in the spiritual power which strangely changed the first Christians, and which has carried Christianity across the world and across the centuries despite the many Christian failures. Other signs of the victory of Jesus lie in our personal history. When we have lived in accordance with the teaching of Jesus, our own lives have been touched by the same power. What we have already seen in the Christian saints and even experienced in our own lives—however imperfectly—leads us to think that in what he said about the pattern of Earth's history Jesus was essentially right.

The Pharisees once asked him, 'When will the kingdom

of God come?' He is reported to have replied: 'You cannot tell by observation when the kingdom comes. There will be no saying, "Look, here it is!" or "there it is!"; for in fact the kingdom of God is among you.' This saying, like many other sayings of Jesus, can be interpreted in more than one way. Probably it meant originally that the full coming of the kingdom of God would be obvious when it did come—as a lightning-flash lights up the earth from end to end (the comparison used in the very next few sentences of Luke's gospel). But the rebuke given to any attempt to treat some ambiguous event controversially as the coming of God's kingdom has rightly encouraged many Christian generations to concentrate on what is sure in their own experience: the coming of God's kingdom through the power of Jesus after his death in his Church and in their own lives. This concentration on spiritual reality has, indeed, led some Christians to prefer the translation of the saying of Jesus which states that 'the kingdom of God is *within* you'. However, the attempt to give an entirely psychological meaning to the idea of the kingdom of God is out of keeping with the rest of Jesus's teaching. This kingdom was to come not only in men's hearts, but completely 'on Earth'. It is now to be seen not only by looking in the history books, and not only by looking in the mirror, but also by watching television—if it is to be seen at all.

The question about the basic truth of the vision of Jesus therefore depends partly on one's verdict on the spiritual results of Christianity and partly on one's estimate of one's personal experience—but the question remains, how one understands the development of the world. It may be thought that the history, and particularly the modern history, of the world is so ambiguous that it is wrong to link it with the idea of the coming of the kingdom of God. In that case, it is of course wise to refrain from saying, 'Look, here it is!' But it may be thought that there is much to be admired in the development of the modern world—and much to thank God for, if one believes in God. In that case, the development which we admire, despite all its continuing tragedy, can be regarded as part of the fulfilment of the promises made by the prophets of ancient Israel and by Jesus; and today's newspaper can be read like a supplement to the Bible, recording God's new acts.

It seems more reasonable for a Christian to take the attitude that the development of the modern world *is* a step in the coming of the kingdom of God—one of the greatest steps yet, although there will be other and greater steps in the thousands of millions of years ahead. Of course God as the ultimate source of this development is hidden from our view, but he is apparently absent only in order that we may have our opportunity. Of course there have been many modern tragedies, and worse ones seem likely. Modern men cut themselves off from each other, spending more on armaments than on education or health (the last analysed world expenditure on armaments came close to the amounts spent on education and health *together*). And many modern men ignore God in practice; some very influential modern men deny him in theory also. Life in such times is testing, perhaps crucifying, for those who seek to serve God's purposes for the world. But the slow process of the world's development continues as humble people are given more and more solid grounds of joy. May it not be the case that the kingdom of God is among us?

Whatever our opinion of the tragic and exhilarating development of the modern world may be, we can at least agree that the original message of Jesus was linked with this world's development far more closely than it was linked with any speculation about a supernatural 'other' world. Indeed, Jesus dismissed such speculation, as is shown by the story about his answer to the riddle of whose wife 'at the resurrection' a woman would be when in this life she had married seven brothers one after the other. 'When they rise from the dead, men and women do not marry; they are like the angels in heaven.' The reason why he did believe in, and clearly teach, the reality of eternal life (using the conventional images of his day such as 'angels', 'Paradise', 'Abraham's bosom') was that he believed in, and clearly taught, the power of God, who was no figure of the imagination. God had the power to bring his rule to Earth 'as it is in heaven'. But even in death the Father would not abandon his children. For God also had the power—beyond anything mortal men and women could understand—to remain after the end of life on earth 'not the God of the dead but of the living'. In the last book of the Bible, one of the early Christians rightly interpreted this promise of a 'new Earth' and a new city in the ultimate splendour as being part of the divine promise to develop the old Earth and to 'make all things new'.[2]

[2] I have offered a rather longer treatment of the Bible's teaching on eternal life in *The Last Things Now* (SCM Press, 1969).

IX

GOD AND EVIL

I

We must make either good our problem, or evil. However, most people would have to think hard in order to imagine what life would look like if the good in it were regarded as the oddity needing explanation. By some sort of instinct, we take for granted the beauty surrounding us, our frequent moments of intense joy, and the generally agreeable nature of life. Almost all of us are glad to be alive. Peasants often seem to be happier than civilized citizens, oppressed people often nurse a sense of dignity and hope, desperately sick people almost always fight for life, there is some laughter in the streets of Calcutta, and very old people do not normally ask to be killed. It is our instinct to cling to life because life is on the whole good for us. This instinct is, as we have seen, the basic religious sense. Our intuition is that the universe has a pattern, and that this pattern is usually favourable to us. Our fulfilment in happiness is part of the thrust of existence. We rejoice and we give thanks—how, is a problem to which poetry and music may be the best answers; why and to whom, it is the business of religion to say.

If we regard life as mainly good—and we do for most of the time—then evil becomes the interloper, and we mean by that every kind of evil. We ask not why Earth supports life, but why there are cyclones; not why man has evolved from other animals, but why he still keeps his appendix; not why there is pleasure, but why there is pain. For religious believers the problem becomes why the ultimate reality—which we must regard as good although it is better than we can imagine—at present co-exists with evil. For believers in God, the problem becomes why the good Creator has made a world which is partly evil. If we have striven to establish personal relationships with God in prayer, we feel let down as if by a friend. People who care about God's honour ask imploringly or indignantly why he does not vindicate himself. More normal people ask pathetically: 'Why has it happened to me, or to my friend, or to my family? We've never done any harm to God.' And some people grow to hate the very idea of God.

Christians are among those who continue to say that the divine reality is single, and who cling to the idea of the sovereign Father, despite the reality of evil. Even more than the prophet Amos who believed that evil could not befall a city unless the Lord had 'done it'—and even more than Jeremiah who had to apply this insight to the fall of Jerusalem itself—Christians have a problem. On the one hand, the founder of Christianity accepted the great Jewish tradition about God the Father, gave it an intensely personal vividness in his prayer to *Abba*, and communicated his vision of the Father with unforgettable power. Jesus believed in God the Father's sovereignty to the extent of saying that no sparrow fell without his permission. On the other hand, Jesus lived as a poor man amid people who were poverty-stricken, disease-ridden and fearful, in an outlying corner of the Roman Empire. He himself knew exhaustion, tears and a bitter gloom in the course of his work for his people, sweated in a torment of anxiety, and was tortured to death by Jerusalem's rubbish-dump, crying in his last agony, 'My God, my God, why hast thou forsaken me?' It necessarily follows from the history of Jesus that the problem of evil is very real. The pretence that human life is not partly tragic is absolutely impossible for Christians.

How are Christians to reconcile their joy in the presence of the Father with their grief in the presence of the cross? How are they to offer any solution for this problem of evil, which their faith has heightened for them, it would seem intolerably? Various attempts have been made to philosophize in this strikingly uncomfortable situation. Very briefly, we may say that these arguments attempt to mitigate the problem of evil by showing that many things which appear to be evil are in deepest reality not so, or are not so completely.

Three main arguments have been advanced. The first is that if anything exists in any distinction from God, it must be less than perfect. As recent philosophers have put it, contingent existence must include an element of Non-Being. The creation must therefore contain evil, if only because it fails to reach the supreme good and to be perfect in 'measure, form, and order'. If we enjoy the creation on the whole, we must take the not so good along with the good. We are not entitled to complain that conditions are not perfect. For example, if animals enjoy life on the whole, we are not entitled to complain that they may need to kill and eat other animals in order to live. If we have the advantage over other animals in being specially sensitive, we are not entitled to protest when we feel more pain.

The second argument which tries to cut down the problem of evil does admit rather more fully that evil really *is* evil. Evil is a definite corruption of the good; it is utterly hostile to God and to God's good creation. So to speak, evil is not merely an imperfect tomato; evil is a squishy, mouldering tomato. But this argument claims that most of the evil which is thus acknowledged to be bad in itself is useful. If a tomato did not go bad, we should not know when to throw it away. More seriously, if fire did not burn our skin, we should not be alarmed and we should destroy ourselves. If evil ways of living did not carry the penance of suffering, we should not feel ourselves obliged to try to live honourably. This is an argument which, stated like that, is naïve, but it can be elaborated in Christian philosophy so as to advocate the acceptance of order as the framework of life, despite its occasional inconvenience—and the acceptance of pain as a warning signal. It can even be worked out so as to present some ghastly road or air accidents as bloodstained signs warning against carelessness; or so as to justify some of the suffering inflicted by war as the only way of teaching people as stupid and cruel as we are to tolerate our neighbours.

The third argument which has been used in the attempt to reason about evil in a creation ruled by the Creator admits more fully still that much evil cannot be justified in its immediate consequences and cannot be explained as a warning to keep to the good path. Much pain, for example, comes too late to warn us; otherwise, no smoker would risk lung cancer. But this third argument suggests that our endurance of evil is necessary in order that our characters may be strengthened. In particular, the reality of evil, horrible and irrational as evil is, calls forth heroic courage, practical compassion, and sacrificial love. Suffering improves humanity in the long run; even wars and cancer hospitals show this. This argument concludes that in the end God will be able to justify all the evil which he has permitted, because without that evil the good end would have been less good. This world, with its mixture of good and evil, will then be understood as a 'vale of soul-making'.

These are powerful arguments, which have been advanced by profound and brilliant thinkers. The first looks to the origin of things; the second looks to the purpose of things as they are; and the third looks to the end of things. Each of these arguments has a considerable validity, and taken together they go far to explain the apparently inexplicable fact that God the sovereign Father allows evil in his creation. But we know that these arguments do not cover everything: they do not cover our own experience of extreme evil. These arguments appear impertinently glib, coldly insensitive and cruelly irrelevant in Auschwitz or Hiroshima, or on the scene of a great natural disaster—and in the age created by the mass media many millions of people have to bear the burden of being vividly aware of such public tragedies. And such arguments do not console in the private tragedies actually experienced in our age as in any other. They may be relevant, but they do not feel true beside a corpse. We cannot help thinking that the good God might have planned a creation containing less evil to be permitted, a moral gymnasium with fewer instruments of torture. As a part of the agony of it, we cannot help asking ourselves whether the good God planned it at all, or whether

> As flies to wanton boys, are we to the gods,
> They kill us for their sport.

These arguments have another deficiency. Although they have been used by many Christians, not one of them derives from specifically Christian convictions. We ask, therefore, whether it is not possible to go more deeply into the tragedy, and find a definitely Christian answer to the problem of evil. That means that we must look again at Jesus himself.

2

Jesus was a man of masterful silences. He taught by what he refused to say as much as by what he did say, and his wisest followers have refused to put Christianity at stake in controversies where the Master himself refused to be judge. Jesus refused to pontificate about a theoretical solution to the problem of evil, and our verdict after many centuries of philosophical theology may be that the Master's silence was wisest here too. But we should ourselves be fools if we despised the struggles of Christian philosophers to reason about evil; and although Jesus was no philosopher, his very refusals to teach certain well-known theories are significant.

The first great refusal made by Jesus was his refusal to pronounce about the origins of evil. This silence comes as a surprise to many Christians who know that Jesus shared the beliefs of his contemporaries in Satan and demons, and that Paul, and later theologians, held mythological theories about the original perfection of the creation, about the Falls of the angels and of Adam, and about the consequences for mankind and for nature, which were believed to be now partially under the control of Satan. But no speculation about the origins of evil is recorded as coming from Jesus. On the contrary, it is typical of Jesus that when he tells his story of the weeds among the wheat he is vague about who is to blame for the weeds. 'A man sowed his field with good seed; but while everyone was asleep his enemy came, sowed darnel among the wheat, and made off.' John conveys the impatience of Jesus with speculation in this conversation. Question: 'Rabbi, who sinned, this man or his parents? Why was he born blind?' Answer: 'It is not that this man or his parents sinned; he was born blind so that God's power might be displayed in curing him.'

The second great refusal made by Jesus was his refusal to say that in this life evil always comes to the person who is specially wicked. Jesus fully accepted the fact of a moral order above and around men, but he would not pretend that the good man always prospers and the evil man always suffers; indeed, he repeatedly warned his hearers not to be facile in separating good from bad, wheat from weeds, before God's judgement was clear.

Jesus made a commonsensical appeal to everyday experience. The Galileans who happened to be killed when Pilate's soldiers charged the crowd in the Temple had not been greater sinners than anyone else in Galilee. The eighteen people who were killed when the tower fell on them at Siloam were not more guilty than anyone else in Jerusalem. The good man does not get more sunshine than his bad neighbour. We should let our minds absorb this remarkable refusal to say that righteousness is always rewarded in the order which now exists on the earth, because many Christians have not been so careful. This is the reticence of a teacher who believed that before God all men were guilty and deserved to perish if they did not repent. No one could accuse Jesus of being amoral. But precisely those facts which have seemed to many to be facts counting against the rule of the good God were to him illustrations of the sovereign Father's mercy on a sinful mankind. God in his mercy had refrained from killing everyone off, or starving them to death; that was why some Galileans escaped from the sword and why some dishonest farmers enjoyed good crops. The parables of Jesus constantly depicted God as putting the fact of his Fatherhood of men above their follies and above the conventional division of men into good and bad. And what Jesus preached about God he practised as God's agent; he insisted on table-fellowship with prostitutes and swindlers.

Jesus, then, refused to blame the angels' sin, or Adam's sin, or the individual's sin for all suffering. And the third great refusal made by Jesus was his refusal to say that suffering always improves the character. In the first chapter of Mark, we do not read that the epileptic was exhorted to have patience; we read that the epileptic was cured. We do not read that Simon Peter's mother-in-law was encouraged to have beautiful thoughts in bed; we read that Jesus helped her to her feet. We read that 'he healed many who suffered from various diseases'. It was part of what was involved in proclaiming the message that 'the kingdom of God is upon you'. Jesus accepted tribulations as sent by God; he accepted his cross, and warned his followers that they would have to do the same. But he was totally unsentimental about suffering. He knew that while it made some souls it destroyed others. He told the women of Jerusalem to weep for themselves and their children, and he told his followers to pray that they should not be tested too severely. Evil was in the world. It was not to be explained by tracing its origins; it was not to be justified as the punishment of the bad; it was not to be tolerated as always good for people. Evil was to be accepted as a fact—as an enemy, as a mystery, as a danger; and evil was to be fought.

If this is what Jesus said about evil, or rather refused to say, does not his silence put a question to all those Christians who have been too eloquent in their philosophies of evil? And does it not liberate us from the humbug which has too often accompanied pious people's attempts to edify those who suffer? It is surely a point in favour of the Christian vision of life if this vision is unblinkingly realistic. It is surely honourable to brush aside the drugs as one goes to one's cross.

3

In the Book of Job, in the Old Testament, the sufferer stops complaining when he is shown the crocodile. In the New Testament, the sufferer stops complaining when he is shown the cross. In both cases there is one similarity: the endless debate about the problem of evil is not resolved intellectually but is cut short by a fresh experience, by an event in which ultimate reality is felt to be disclosed. For the Book of Job, ultimate reality is power:

the power of the transcendent One who created all that is, who is more powerful than the most powerful of his creatures, who is not to be questioned about his creation in terms of human morality. When Job sees the crocodile, he is reminded of the doctrine that the clay should not indulge in backchat with the Potter. But for the New Testament, ultimate reality is love. Here is the love of the Father who created out of love, who controls by the force of love, who has placarded his love in the death of Jesus for our sake. The Christian answer to the problem of evil is the cross. That is, the Christian finds assurance in his bewilderment about ultimate reality, and finds strength for his battle with evil, by sharing the humility of Jesus, the fellowship of the sufferings of Jesus, and the power of the victory of Jesus. That is, the Christian finds God on the cross, the Potter covered with clay.

What, more precisely, does the Christian mean? Often in the New Testament the humility of Jesus is commended to us as an example. Jesus accepted a hard life and a cruel death in an evil world, but not without an inner struggle; as the Letter to Hebrews puts it, 'in the days of his earthly life he offered up prayers and petitions, with loud cries and tears, to God who was able to deliver him from the grave', and 'he learned obedience in the school of suffering'. Without explaining the power of evil, Jesus humbly accepted it. The sheer fact of his acceptance has held a lesson of supreme importance for all Christians who have been enrolled in the same tough school. It is, of course, a very shameful fact that Christians have been among the most brutally violent men in history, but such nominal Christians have not been disciples of Jesus. His true disciples have learned from Jesus not to waste energy by complaining. They have also learned from their Master on his cross not to retaliate against evil by fighting with evil weapons; not even to curse back. They have learned how to endure suffering in silence, and how to soak up evil as a sponge soaks up water, until in the end the power of evil is broken because there is nothing more for evil to do. That is picture-language, but it describes the historical Jesus and it also describes the constantly repeated Christian experience. Christians have slowly learned to abandon the notion—common in the Old Testament, for example—that earthly prosperity must be a sign of God's favour. Instead they have heard from Jesus the astonishing warnings against riches and those equally astonishing announcements about who are the lucky ones:

> How blest are you who are in need . . .
> How blest are you who now go hungry . . .
> How blest are you who weep now . . .
> How blest you are when men hate you . . .

Jesus sees no alternative to the cup of suffering for himself, and no alternative to the way of the cross for any who would follow him. This is not only because life must be hard at times for everyone in this partly evil world; it is also because life must be specially hard for those who try to obey God in the world. Jesus calls us to discipleship, imitating his obedience to God, and tells us that the cost of discipleship will be like a cross. Countless Christians have found consolation and encouragement in the thought of this fellowship to which they belong, this noble army into which they have been recruited perhaps without realizing much about what was happening. They have been able to put it very simply: 'What was good enough for Jesus and the saints is good enough for me.' And, looking back over all the centuries of suffering, including the cross of Jesus, they have been able to see something hidden from Jesus as he died.

On his cross Jesus felt that his Father had forsaken him, for Jesus shared the mental as well as the physical sufferings of mankind. But in reality, as Christians have come to see it, the Father was there on Calvary. God the Father was acting mightily in the whole life of Jesus, and that divine action came to its climax when the life of Jesus was summed up in his death. In a way which Christians have seen and experienced but have never been able to understand, the eternal God, the Source and Goal of all, was specially and uniquely involved in the life of Jesus including his suffering and his dying. God was involved personally, not by using an ambassador; yet God was involved without ceasing to be God, without ceasing to be perfect in eternal peace and joy. Although for centuries Christian theologians because of their reverence fought shy of saying that God the Father can suffer, Christian devotion has not scrupled to dwell on the 'Passion of God the Son' and to sing of the 'love divine' which is surveyed as Jesus dies in the utmost degradation. In modern times, more and more Christian theologians have had the courage to agree that because of his love God suffers, although always in such a way that the peace and joy of God's eternal being are not overcome. God is of the company of those who suffer; and in all their affliction he is afflicted. He is, as T. S. Eliot wrote, the 'wounded surgeon'.

Seeing that this is his method of working, Christians now believe that God the Father accepts responsibility for his creation in a way which they can recognize as moral. God does not share his sovereignty with other powers, however conceived; nor does he exercise his sovereignty in a way which must outrage our sense of morality. He is in control, and he is working his good purpose out. But there is a price to be paid in order that his purpose for his creation may be fulfilled. He is morally entitled to call on his creatures to pay that price—because he is willing to pay it himself by suffering. In his last will and testament,

George Bernard Shaw permitted himself a sneer at the cross but stated that he believed in 'creative evolution'. To Christians, the self-disclosure of the suffering God on the cross is what enables a moral man to believe that evolution has a pattern put there by the good Creator.

And according to Christians, God now assures his creatures that beyond the suffering lies triumph. In the Easter experience, Christians have glimpsed the world as God means it to be; a world where a heartbroken Mary is consoled, where a shamefaced Peter is forgiven, where friends on a road walk into the banquet of God's kingdom, where peace and power flood into God's frightened children from their eternal source. Christians are people who cannot forget that glimpse of destiny. And Christians are people who know that the endurance of evil is essential to the completion of the glory they have glimpsed. That is the significance of the wounds which are reported to have been seen remaining in the extremely mysterious 'risen' body at the centre of the Easter experiences. Now the worst that man could do to frustrate the good purpose of God is taken into, and made part of, that purpose; 'partial evil' is transfigured into 'universal good', although at a price which no eighteenth-century optimist could conceive. Now we can give a Christian, instead of a complacent, meaning to Augustine's great saying that 'God judged it better to bring good out of evil than to allow no evil to exist'. Now even that Friday can be called Good, and the evil which caused it can be described (as it was in the old Roman service on the eve of Easter) as a 'happy fault', because it brought about such a rescue.

X

IN PRACTICE

Jesus preferred the young man who refused to do a day's work, but afterwards went quietly and did it, to his brother who declared 'I go, sir'—and did not go. Far too much time has been spent by Christians on discussion, argument and bitter dispute about exactly what it means to say 'sir' to God the Father, or to Jesus himself. The most important consequence of responding to the self-disclosure of God through Jesus must always be to go to work in the world which God is developing.

Jesus made great promises to his few followers. 'Have no fear, little flock; for your Father has chosen to give you the kingdom.' None of his teaching suggests that in the twentieth century it would be his wish that this 'flock' should be scattered for ever. On the contrary, the experience shows that it is vital for the followers of Jesus to keep in touch with each other—and with him through each other. In practice, a solitary Christian is likely to wither away. But all the teaching of Jesus shows that his followers are utterly wrong to concentrate on their own togetherness, or on their claims or anxieties about their emotions. At the beginning their task was clear, and nothing has altered it. They were to make their practical contributions, and these were to be tokens of their message. They were to explain the coming of the kingdom of God. Luke's gospel declares that when Jesus called 'the Twelve' together, he sent them 'to proclaim the kingdom of God and to heal'. When he appointed a further seventy-two messengers, the instruction was repeated: 'Heal the sick . . . and say, "The kingdom of God has come close to you".'

The Father had chosen to give the kingdom to the 'little flock', but not only to them. All the nations were summoned to the feast. What *was* given to the little flock, and to them only, was the news that the kingdom was coming —and the obligation to pass on the news as the interpretation of the world's development.

Far too much time has been spent on talk and quarrels about the precise relationship between Jesus and his followers. Jesus identified himself with his followers by asking that they should be regarded as his family. Looking round at those who were sitting in the circle about him, while his own mother and brothers were outside the house wanting to see him, he said: 'Here are my mother and my brothers. Whoever does the will of God is my brother, my sister, my mother.' But even that great charter of the Christian Church was qualified by the insistence on *doing*. And the followers of Jesus, when they have really followed, have always known this—and have known, too, that others beside them did the will of God.

The recognition of the supremacy of the practical can be illustrated from the history of the interpretation of the parable of the last judgement. This parable was given towards the end of Matthew's gospel as the climax of all the parables. It told of the judgement pronounced by 'the King' on 'all the nations' at the close of history. Those who had fed, befriended and clothed 'one of my brothers here' were told that 'you did it for me'. When this story was first told, almost certainly these 'brothers' were the followers of Jesus. In other words, the nations were being judged on their treatment of the Church. Thus the original meaning of this parable was identical with the saying of Jesus to his followers, also given by Matthew: 'To receive you is to receive me, and to receive me is to receive the One who sent me . . . if anyone gives so much as a cup of cold water to one of these little ones, because he is a disciple of mine . . . that man will assuredly not go unrewarded.' Here the 'little one' receiving the cup of cold water, not the man giving it, was the disciple.

But in the Church from an early date, a broader interpretation has been given to the parable—as to the saying about the cup of cold water. This makes the 'brothers' who need befriending not merely Christians but anyone in need. In other words, the nations are now being judged on their treatment of the poor. For new questions have been asked. Can those who have had no real opportunity to become Christians, or who have been put off Christianity by the faults of Christians, be counted among the 'righteous'? Can those who have certainly never seen Jesus, and who perhaps have never seen a true Christian, serve Jesus and the coming kingdom of God? And the right answer to those questions has been clear to many Christians. Every kind act in history counts ultimately as if it had been done to Jesus in person. All compassion is part of Christianity.

Jesus, as understood by the Church, has thus identified himself not only with the Church but also with all who suffer. He has blessed not only the faith of the Church but also all the goodness of the world. Whoever 'dwells in love' dwells in God, as John saw; it is only the unloving who know nothing of God. And in this understanding, the Church was not false to the teaching of the historical Jesus. With his time so limited, Jesus devoted his energies to his mission to his fellow-Jews and to the training of his followers. But incidents showed that he looked forward to the involvement of all the nations in the drama of the kingdom which he announced and began. When a Phoenician woman made the witty remark that the Gentiles were like dogs under the table entitled to the children's scraps, he was delighted. When Jesus briefly met a Gentile army officer, he did not examine his theology or preach to him but simply admired his practical sense that some people had authority in healing diseases just as army officers had authority in getting their uniforms cleaned. He then prophesied that 'many will come from east and west to feast with Abraham, Isaac and Jacob'.

Much of the life which Jesus commanded his followers to put into practice was no different from the life of those around them. In his own teaching Jesus constantly repeated the Old Testament, and it is reasonable to think that Christian moral teaching has been right to agree on many points with many non-Christian authorities. This began in the time of the New Testament; the letters to Christians preserved there quote with approval moral teaching widely taught in the ancient world, for example by the Stoic philosophers. The attempts that have been made to find a specifically and exclusively Christian way of behaviour were wrong from the start. And the attempts to lay down a detailed Christian plan for daily life were also mistaken. Even in a moral crisis where he might have been expected to take his own stand, Jesus often disappointed questioners. He refused to arbitrate in a financial dispute. The attempts made by Christians to find *the* Christian answer to all the moral problems thrown up by subsequent generations have therefore often been unsuccessful. There is only one authority which is undeniably Christian: the moral authority of Jesus. And the teaching of Jesus as recorded in the gospels simply does not provide a basis on which one can build *the* Christian solution of political, economic or medical problems. The legacy left by Jesus was not exclusive—and was not complete.

But this is not to say that being a Christian makes no difference at all. The Christian is given spiritual and moral power. This may not always be able to make him nobler than the non-Christian, but it is (as he knows) able to make him better than he himself would have been without Christianity. The power comes through the Christian's faith, or through his vision of life, because the faith or vision calms and encourages him by showing him the power of God already at work in him and in the world. One difference in being a Christian was put simply and clearly in the gospels. 'It has been granted to you to know the secrets of the kingdom of God.' The Christian has an inner peace. But the vision also teases, excites and challenges him, because it inspires him to live now in the light of what is coming.

The moral teachings of Jesus collected by Matthew in the Sermon on the Mount are very strange, although the Sermon on the Mount is often supposed by those who have not read it with care to be a simple summary of everyday commonplaces. These teachings only make sense when we realize to whom these teachings were addressed. Jesus was speaking to 'his disciples', who did know the secrets of the coming kingdom. They knew that the perfect order was on its way, and therefore they were challenged to live now as if it had come. The challenges piled up, next-to-impossible for human beings in the world as it is: never be angry, never have a lustful thought, never retaliate, love and collaborate with your enemies, do not save up, do not worry about food, drink or clothes, pass no judgement. These challenges are simply invitations to live with a greater dignity as human beings. But the humanism held up as the ideal is so heroic that in practice those who have lived on this level have been few. Those who have allowed themselves to be troubled by such ideals have also been a minority. These challenges do not always provide quick answers to the ethical dilemmas of daily life, as many sincere Christians have found. But—as many have also found—they are the morality of the kingdom of God; they belong to the vision of the future, a vision with power over the often sordid or tragic present.

If people can keep that vision or anything like it before them, many wrong choices in everyday decisions can be forgiven. Jesus taught, indeed, that there is only one unforgivable sin: calling the good devilish, the light dark. That sin is unforgivable because that sinner cannot see the good and the light and be healed by them. If that ultimate sin is avoided, people are left to make the best decision they can in each situation they meet: and are forgiven. So understood, Christian morality is marked by a glorious freedom unknown to those who feel bound to obey a moral code. On the other hand, it is haunted by a demand far sterner than the kind of 'love' which is often contrasted with 'law'.

Some critics say that the teaching of Jesus is itself to blame for much of the error and the evil in the history of Christianity, and it certainly is the case that this first-century Jew had a message which was not in all respects identical with twentieth-century humanitarianism. But while some of the critics of the Christian Church frankly class Jesus among the enemies of humanity, most do not. Most people revere this solitary figure—and regret that he is solitary. For them, the tragedy is that so much of historical Christianity has wandered so far from the teaching of Jesus. As an interpretation of human life, Christianity has often been closer to the creed of the unscrupulous merchants described by Jesus in first-century Palestine, and closed still to the worship of the Caesar in whose name Jesus was executed. And historical Christianity has been in some respects identical with the arrogance of the Pharisees and scribes whom Jesus denounced. The worst bitterness about the story of Jesus seems to many people to be this: after his death what he had openly and unforgettably attacked was comfortably established in his name. The Danish rebel, Soren Kierkegaard, remarked that there has been only one Christian, and he died on the cross.

So Christians work in the world alongside people who have never said 'I go, sir' to God through Jesus. And as they struggle to relate their vision of the future to the tragedies and dilemmas around them, Christians pray. To them, prayer is recalling the hope that is in them.

As instructed by him, they make their own the astonishing prayer to *Abba*, Father, which Jesus used. But they never do this in a sentimental way; when they have addressed God as 'Daddy', they instantly recall that because of the mystery surrounding his reality God is to be treated as different from all people and all things, as 'holy'. They look forward with ardent hope to the full coming of the reign of God on the planet Earth, cleansing its bloodstained soil and satisfying minds dismayed by its many evils. And they work for this. Therefore they ask to be given today enough strength to live through the day in the light of that vision of the world's development. In this great hope, they ask that tomorrow may be made real today.[1]

In their prayer Christians ask that forgiveness may cover their many defects, because they forgive, understand and are indebted to their many critics—and because they have not finally abandoned the vision they have seen. And with the humility that comes from a knowledge of their past failures they hope that, in a time of many searching tests, they may not be tested to breaking-point, but may keep the vision.

[1] In the prayer usually translated 'Give us today our daily bread', the Greek word behind 'daily' is strange. After examining the evidence, many scholars believe that in Aramaic, the language used by Jesus and his followers, the word behind the Greek means 'for tomorrow'.